Technical English 2

Course Book

PEARSON
Longman

David Bonamy

Contents

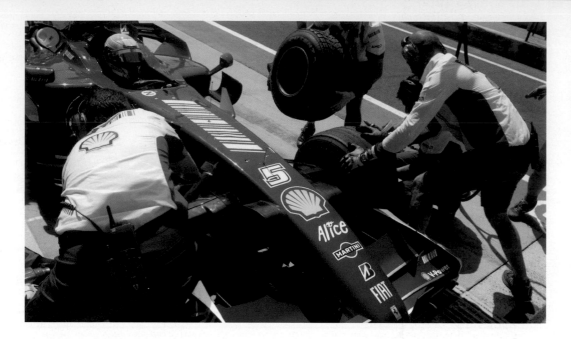

1 Teamwork

Start here **1** Discuss these questions with a partner.

- How many mechanics work in a pit-stop crew in a big race?
  a) about 4   b) about 10   c) about 20
- What jobs do they do? List the most important jobs.

Reading **2** Read this interview with the head of a pit-stop crew. Check your answers to 1.

Making every second count

How do mechanics service a car so quickly in the middle of a car race? Will Peters is chief mechanic and crew leader of a pit-stop crew. Here he explains his work.

I'm the crew leader, and I have twenty mechanics in my crew. It's dangerous work, so we wear fire suits and safety helmets. I have five teams: *wheel-gun*, *wheel-on*, *wheel-off*, *wheel-jack* and *fuel*.

Every second is important in the middle of a race, so everyone moves quickly and works together as a team.

– 30 secs	I give the order: 'Get ready!' The four *wheel-on* mechanics bring out the new wheels. The tyres are still covered in warm blankets. The team leader adjusts the air pressure in the tyres.
– 10 secs	The car enters the pit lane, and slows down. The driver presses a button in his cockpit. This opens the fuel flap.
– 3 secs	The car approaches the garage. I signal to the driver: STOP. The driver slows down and drives towards the crew. The *wheel-gun* team leader signals with his hand, and the driver stops the car next to the wheel guns.

00:00 secs	The four *wheel-gun* mechanics run to the car. They loosen the nuts with their wheel guns. Then they move back quickly.
00:01 secs	The two *wheel-jack* team members run to the car, and place the jacks under the front and rear of the car. They raise the car off the ground and move back quickly.
00:01.5 secs	Then three members of the *fuel* team move forward. One carries the fuel nozzle, and the other two carry the fuel hose. (It weighs 40 kg!). The front fuel mechanic pushes the nozzle into the fuel socket on the car. They then switch on the fuel pump.
00:02 secs	The *wheel-off* mechanics move forward. They take the old wheels off and take them away quickly.
00:02.5 secs	Now the *wheel-on* guys move forward. They take the warm blankets off the new wheels, put the new wheels on the car, and move back quickly. On the other side of the car, another mechanic puts his arm into the cockpit and cleans the driver's visor.
00:03 secs	The *wheel-gun* guys move forward and tighten the nuts. Then they raise a hand to signal that everything is OK.
00:04 secs	The *wheel-jack* people lower the car to the ground and take the jacks away. Now everyone is waiting. The *fuel* guys are still pumping fuel into the car. They hold the fuel nozzle and hose in place until all the fuel is in the car.
00:05.5 secs	I signal to the driver: SELECT FIRST GEAR. He pushes the gear lever into first gear, and waits.
00:06.5 secs	The fuel pump switches off, and the fuel guys pull out the fuel nozzle. Another *fuel* team member cleans spilled fuel off the car, and moves back quickly. Immediately, I signal to the driver: GO.
00:07 secs	The car moves to the end of the pit lane. The driver presses the button to close the fuel flap.
00:10 secs	The car speeds up and leaves the pit lane. It's in the race again.

3 Label the parts.

> flap   hose   jack   nozzle   socket
> wheel gun

4 Complete this checklist of instructions for each team.

TEAM 1: WHEEL-JACK
1 _____ .
2   Raise the car off the ground.
3   WAIT
4 _____ .
5   Take _____ .

TEAM 2: WHEEL-GUN
1   Loosen the wheel nuts on the old wheels.
2   WAIT.
3   Tighten the wheel nuts on the new wheels.
4 _____ .

TEAM 3: WHEEL-OFF
1   Take the old wheels off.
2 _____ .

TEAM 4: WHEEL-ON
1   Bring out the new wheels.
2   Adjust _____ .
3   WAIT.
4   Take the covers _____ .
5 _____ .

TEAM 5: FUEL
1   Push _____ .
2   Pump _____ .
3 _____ .
4 _____ .

2 Training

Start here   **1**   ▶ 🔊 02   You are a trainee pit-stop mechanic. A trainer is giving you instructions. Listen and write numbers 1–10 to show the correct order of instructions.

Tighten the wheel nuts.		Adjust the air pressure in the tyre.	
Raise the car with the jack.		Bring the new wheel out.	
Loosen the wheel nuts.		Put the new wheel on.	
Take the old wheel off.		Put the jack under the car.	
Take the old wheel away.		Lower the car and take the jack away.	

Vocabulary   **2**   Match the pictures with the verbs in the box.

> lift up   pick up   pull out   push in   put down   put on   take away   take off

Language

Imperative	Present continuous	Present perfect
Take the tyres off.	I'm taking the tyres off now.	I've taken the tyres off.
Take off the tyres.	I'm taking off the tyres now.	I've taken off the tyres.
Take them off.	I'm taking them off.	I've taken them off.
Not: ~~Take off them.~~	Not: ~~I'm taking off them.~~	Not: ~~I've taken off them.~~

3   ▶ 🔊 03   Listen and respond to these instructions quickly. Confirm (a) what you are doing and then (b) what you have done.

Example: 1 (You hear) Bring out the new tyres. (You say) Right. I'm bringing them out now. OK, I've brought them out.

4 Work in pairs. Make dialogues between a supervisor (S) and a trainee (T) from the checklists.

1	• put new tyres on • tighten wheel nuts • adjust air pressure	*done* *in progress* *not yet done*	4	• switch off electricity • test all circuits • find any faults	*done* *in progress* *not yet done*	
2	• take cover off • repair computer • take out damaged chip	*done* *in progress* *not yet done*	5	• strip off old paint • plaster holes in wall • buy new paint	*done* *in progress* *not yet done*	
3	• replace burnt wire • switch on power • check other wires	*done* *in progress* *not yet done*	6	• take apart telephone • put it together again • test it	*done* *in progress* *not yet done*	

S: *How are you getting on?*

T: *I've put the new tyres on. I'm still tightening the wheel nuts. It's almost done.*

S: *OK, good. Have you adjusted the air pressure yet?*

T: *No, I haven't done that yet. I'll do it next.*

Phrases to gain more time:
*Hang on. Just a minute.
One minute. Nearly finished.
Almost done.*

Language

yet is used with present perfect questions and negatives to emphasise the period of time up to now.

Has Bill finished that job yet? The speaker wanted or expected Bill to finish the job before now. *John hasn't cleaned the car yet.* The speaker wanted or expected John to clean the car before now.

Task

5 Work in small groups. Choose one of these car jobs. With your group, make a set of instructions for doing the job.

Changing a wheel

Cleaning a spark plug

Checking the oil level

6 Turn to page 111. Find useful instructions from the list. Revise your own set of instructions. Rewrite them if necessary, and make them short and simple.

7 Roleplay this situation with someone from another group with a different job.

Student A. You're the manager of a garage. You're showing a new trainee how to do the job. Tell the trainee how to do the job, but don't look at your set of instructions. Give instructions, and check how the trainee is getting on.
First of all, loosen the wheel nuts. Have you done that yet? Good. Right. Now lift up the car with the jack. OK? Well done.

Student B. You're a new trainee in the garage. Follow the manager's instructions. Mime the actions if you can. Tell the manager how you're getting on.
Hang on. Just a minute. No, not yet. I'm still loosening the wheel nuts. It's almost done. OK, I've finished. I've taken it off. What do I do next?

3 Method

1 How do you start or activate these devices?

2 Complete the sentences.

> break   kick   pick up   press   pull   switch on   touch

1   The passenger activates the ticket machine by _touching_ the screen.
2   You switch on the phone by _____ _____ the handset and _____ the green button.
3   The user starts the outboard motor by _____ the handle of the cord.
4   The rider starts the engine by _____ _____ the battery and _____ the lever downwards.
5   The burglar activates the alarm by _____ the laser beam.

Speaking   **3** Make questions and answers.

A: How does the passenger activate the ticket machine?
B: He activates it / He does it by touching the screen.

Language

	Method	
You start the outboard motor	by pulling	the cord.
The burglar activated the alarm	by breaking	a laser beam.

4 Work in pairs. Match the devices with the methods.

Device
1   accelerator on motorbike
2   voice-operated computer
3   solar battery
4   emergency stop in train
5   shop door alarm
6   car engine

How to start/activate it
a)   put it under an electric lamp
b)   step on a sensor in the door mat
c)   rotate the handle
d)   insert the key and turn it
e)   pull the lever
f)   speak to it

Speaking   **5** Make questions and answers.

A: How do you activate the accelerator on a motorbike?
B: By rotating the handle. (or You activate it by rotating the handle.)

Writing

6 Write sentences explaining how to activate or start the devices in 4.

you, the user, the customer, the driver, the passenger

1 You activate / The user activates the accelerator on a motorbike by rotating the handle.

Reading

7 What can this robot do? How does it work? Discuss with your partner.

8 Read this magazine article. Write the names of the devices in the chart.

MURATA BOY

weighs less than 5 kg and is only 508 mm tall, but it can do something that no other robot can do. It can ride a bike. How does it do this? By means of sensors and wireless technology. One sensor is located in the robot's body. This sensor keeps the robot upright and prevents it from falling sideways. The robot can look ahead using a small camera in its head. The camera helps the robot to ride in a straight line. Another sensor is located in its chest. This sensor prevents it from hitting a wall or other object. The robot can receive instructions from an external computer by means of a wireless receiver in the box on its back. The computer makes it follow the correct road. Finally, if the road is not flat, another sensor (in the frame of the bike) can feel the movement of the wheel. The sensor allows the robot to ride over bumps in the road.

Murata Manufacturing Co Ltd

Murata Boy can do these things	device	location
(1) It can stay in a vertical position on the bike	sensor	body
(2) It can receive instructions from an outside computer		
(3) It can detect changes in the surface of the road		
(4) It can look straight ahead and move straight forward		
(5) It can detect walls and move away from them		

Language

The robot can look ahead	by using by using by means of	a camera in its head.

Speaking

9 Supply the questions for this interview with the inventor of the robot.

1 A: *What* _____?
   B: It can ride a bicycle.
2 A: *How* _____?
   B: It works by means of sensors and wireless technology.
3 A: _____?
   B: By means of a sensor in the frame of the bike.
4 A: _____?
   B: By a sensor in its chest.
5 A: _____?
   B: By using a camera.

1 Routines

Start here 1 Would you like to work on an offshore oil platform? Why/Why not? Discuss with a partner.

Listening 2 ▶ 04 Tore and Ken work on different oil platforms. Listen to their phone call and complete the information on the left.

TORE	
ON DUTY: ____ weeks.	
ON LEAVE: ____ weeks.	

KEN	
ON DUTY: ____ weeks.	
ON LEAVE: ____ weeks.	

3 Listen to Tore (T) and Ken (K) again and complete the conversation.

T: *Hi, Ken. How are things on your rig?*
K: Hi, Tore. Well, we (1) _____ very hard at the moment. But I (2) _____ on leave tomorrow.
T: *That's great. Where (3) _____? Back home?*
K: I usually (4) _____ home to Nigeria. But this time I (5) _____ to France for a holiday.
T: *Ah, fantastic. (6) _____ two weeks on, two weeks off?*
K: No, I (7) _____ three on and three off. How about you?
T: *I (8) _____ two two.*
K: When's your next leave?
T: *I'm on the helicopter right now! I (9) _____ to Norway!*

onshore ≠ offshore
on duty ≠ off duty
on leave = on holiday

Language The present simple is used to talk about (1) regular or routine events; (2) job descriptions; (3) processes

The present continuous is used to talk about (1) things happening now; (2) things happening temporarily around now; (3) plans or intentions for the near future.

Speaking 4 Work in pairs. Ask each other about the changes in the work routine.

A: *What does Tore usually do from six to seven forty-five?*
B: *He usually supervises the deck crew. But not today.*
A: *What's he doing today?*
B: *He's operating the main crane.*

Changes to Monday morning duty roster for today only (because of staff illness)			
	06.00–07.45	08.00–09.45	10.00–10.45
BILL	~~inspect underwater pipes~~ check diving equipment	~~supervise divers~~ inspect blowout preventer	~~conduct safety drill~~ attend safety meeting
TORE	~~supervise deck crew~~ operate main crane	~~operate main crane~~ train new deck crew	~~work in control room~~ work on deck
ADEL	~~check generators~~ repair power line	~~do maintenance work~~ supervise electricians	~~test electrical switches~~ write safety report

5 ▶ 💿 05 Listen to these oil rig workers talking about their jobs. Tick their jobs on the organisation charts.

BILL	TORE	KEN	ADEL
SUB-SEA CREW	**DECK CREW**	**DRILL CREW**	**ELECTRICAL DEPARTMENT**
Sub-Sea Engineer ↓ Assistant Sub-Sea Engineer	Crane Operator ↓ Assistant Crane Operator · Roustabout	Driller ↓ Assistant Driller ↓ Derrick Man · Pump Man	Maintenance Supervisor ↓ Chief Electrician ↓ Electrician

6 Complete the job descriptions. Use the correct form of these verbs.

maintain operate repair report supervise

1 The Assistant Sub-Sea Engineer _repairs_ and _____ the platform and the pipes under the sea. He _____ to the Sub-Sea Engineer.
2 The Assistant Crane Operator _____ and _____ the cranes on the main deck. He _____ to the Crane Operator.
3 The Assistant Driller _____ the drilling equipment. He _____ the Derrick Man and the Pump Man. He _____ to the Driller.
4 The Chief Electrician _____ and _____ all the electrical equipment on the rig. He _____ three electricians. He _____ to the Maintenance Supervisor.

Speaking **7** Work in pairs. Act the parts of two of the oil rig workers. Ask each other about your jobs.

What's your job? What do you do?
I'm an Assistant Driller. I operate the drilling equipment.
Do you supervise anyone? Who do you supervise? Who reports to you?
Who do you report to? Who supervises you?

8 Write down your job title and a short job description. If you do not have a job, think of a job you want when you finish all your training.

9 Work in pairs. Ask each other about your jobs.

2 Plans

1 What jobs does a safety officer on an offshore oil platform have to do? Discuss with your partner.

2 ▶ 🎵 06 Ben is a safety officer on an oil rig. Listen to his phone call. What is the purpose of the call?

a) to discuss safety rules   c) to arrange a meeting

b) to talk about the strong wind

Day: _____

Time: _____

Participants: _____

_____

Agenda: _____

_____

3 Listen to the phone call again and complete these notes.

4 Listen to Tore (T) and Ben (B) again and fill in the gaps.

T: *Hello, Deck Crew. Tore speaking.*

B: Oh, hi Tore. This is Ben. How's it going?

T: *Not bad. But this strong wind is a problem for the cranes. Anyway, what can I do for you?*

B: I (1) _____ hold a meeting for the deck crew sometime soon.

T: *OK. What's the meeting (2) _____ be about?*

B: I (3) _____ tell them about the new safety rules for crane operators.

T: *OK, that's fine. When (4) _____ the meeting?*

B: How about three o'clock next Thursday?

T: *Yeah, that's great. Three o'clock next Thursday. See you then. Bye.*

B: Cheers. Bye.

Language   The present continuous, or *going to* + verb, is used to talk about plans or intentions. *I'm holding / I'm going to hold a meeting next Thursday.*

to is used after verbs such as *plan, want, intend, hope. I want / intend / hope to finish this report next week.*

---

5 You are Ben and this is your diary for this week. Explain your plans.

MON	(1) 09.30 meet safety manager – discuss safety report
	(2) 14.00 take helicopter to HQ – meet company manager
TUE	(3) 12.00 write new safety rules for cranes
WED	(4) 08.00 inspect fire exits (5) 10.00 run fire drill
	(6) 14.00 visit Nord Platform – discuss new safety rules with manager
THU	(7) – day off!
FRI	(8) 09.30 write report about visit to Nord Platform
	(9) 14.00 inspect sub-sea safety equipment

Example: On Monday at 9.30, I'm meeting the safety manager. We're going to discuss the safety report.

6 Ask Ben questions about his diary.

Example: When are you meeting the safety manager? What are you going to discuss?

Task **7** What things do you have to do today (or at the weekend)? Make a list, and then work out a timetable for doing them. Present your plan to the class.

Writing **8** Rewrite this email replacing the phrases in italics.

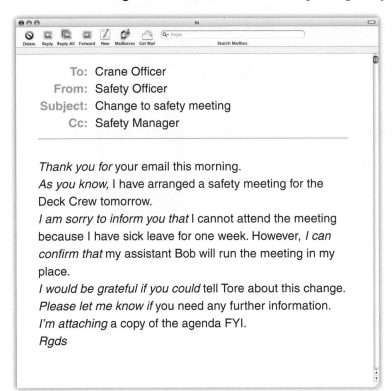

Thanking for communication	*Thanks for; Many thanks for*
Referring to topic	*With reference to; With regard to; Concerning*
Reminding of background	*As you are aware,; As you may know,; As you may be aware,*
Confirming something	*This is to confirm that; I'd like to confirm that; I confirm that*
Introducing bad news	*I am sorry to tell you that; Unfortunately,*
Introducing good news	*I am pleased to inform you that; Fortunately,*
Giving new information	*I would like to inform you that; This is to let you know that*
Requesting action	*Please; Could you please; I would appreciate it if you could*
Showing you are available	*Please do not hesitate to contact me if; Do let me know if*
Attaching document	*I attach*
Closing	*Kind regards; Regards; Best wishes; Best*

Email content:

To: Crane Officer
From: Safety Officer
Subject: Change to safety meeting
Cc: Safety Manager

Thank you for your email this morning.
As you know, I have arranged a safety meeting for the Deck Crew tomorrow.
I am sorry to inform you that I cannot attend the meeting because I have sick leave for one week. However, *I can confirm that* my assistant Bob will run the meeting in my place.
I would be grateful if you could tell Tore about this change.
Please let me know if you need any further information.
I'm attaching a copy of the agenda FYI.
Rgds

9 Write this email.

FYI = for your information

You are Pete Norman, the Manager of Safety World. The company makes and sells safety equipment for oil rigs. You receive an email from Ben Brenner, Safety Officer on Nord Oil Platform. Ben asks if you have any new safety equipment for emergency escapes from oil platforms. Reply to Ben.

- thank Ben for his email yesterday
- refer to his request
- confirm you have new emergency escape equipment for sale
- remind Ben: Safety World is Europe's largest manufacturer of oil safety equipment
- give new information: Safety World won the International Safety Award last year
- request action: send information about safety needs on Nord
- show you are available to answer any of Ben's questions
- attach photos of equipment in action

10 Exchange emails with a partner. Take the part of Ben, and reply to your partner's email.
- thank for email
- remind Pete: there was a serious fire on an oil platform last year; there were many casualties because of poor escape equipment
- give information about needs: you want new fire and emergency escape equipment such as heat shields, heat-resistant ropes, ladders, enough for crew of 230
- ask Pete to send catalogue for these items

3 New job

Start here **1** Have you ever written a CV? What information goes into it?

Reading **2** Read this section of a CV and answer the questions below.

CURRICULUM VITAE		
PERSONAL INFORMATION		
Surname(s) / First name(s)	PETERSONS Anna	
DESIRED EMPLOYMENT	Senior Audio Maintenance Technician	1
WORK EXPERIENCE		
Dates	September 2006 – present day	2
Occupation or position held	Audio maintenance technician	3
Main activities and responsibilities	Maintain digital audio equipment, make recordings, do troubleshooting and repairs, buy new equipment	4
Name and address of employer	Omega Studios, Riga, Latvia	5
Type of business or sector	Electronics, entertainment, media	6
WORK EXPERIENCE		
Dates	2003 – 2005	7
Occupation or position held	Technician	8
Main activities and responsibilities	Repair video and DVD equipment	9
Name and address of employer	Comet Electronics, Riga, Latvia	10
Type of business or sector	Electronics	11
EDUCATION AND TRAINING		
Dates	2005 – 2006	12
Title of qualification awarded	Diploma in Audio Technology	13
Principal subjects/occupational skills covered	Audio electronics, studio equipment, digital audio technology, editing, acoustics	14
Name and type of organisation providing education and training	Thames Valley University, London, UK	15

CV = Curriculum Vitae

1	What is Anna's surname?	5	Where did she work in 2004?
2	What job does she want to have?	6	What were her responsibilities then?
3	Where does Anna work now?	7	What qualification does Anna have?
4	What is her job description?	8	Where did she study?

Scanning **3** Practise your speed reading. Look for the information you need on the SPEED SEARCH pages (118–119). Try to be the first to complete the task.

Task: Find an advert for a job relevant to Anna's career plans, qualifications and work experience.

Listening **4** Anna is talking about her CV. Fill in the gaps.

From 2003 until 2005, I (1) _____ at Comet Electronics as a technician. I (2) _____ Comet in 2005 and (3) _____ a full-time student at Thames Valley University in September 2005. From 2005 to 2006, I (4) _____ audio electronics at Thames Valley. In 2006, I (5) _____ my Diploma in Audio Technology. Then in September 2006, I (6) _____ work as an audio maintenance technician at Omega Studios.

5 ▶ 🔊 07 Listen to Anna, and check your answers.

6 Put these headings in the coloured boxes.

adjective   college subject   equipment   person   scientific concept

	noun				
1	en gin <u>eer</u>	<u>en</u> gine	en gin <u>eer</u> ing		
2	el ec tri cian			el ec tri ci ty	el ec tric al
3			el ec tron ics	el ec tron	el ec tron ic
4	mech an ic	mech an is m	mech an ics		mech an ic al
5	tech ni cian				tech ni cal
6	tech no lo gist		tech no lo gy		

7 Underline the stressed syllables in the words in the white boxes.

8 ▶ 💿 08 Listen and check your answers to 7.

9 Fill in the gaps.

1 The _____ is responsible for every _____ in the factory.
(engineering/engineer/engine)

2 I'm a _____, but I want to become a _____ engineer.
(mechanical/mechanic/mechanics)

3 The lab _____ maintains all the _____ equipment.
(technician/technical/technology)

4 The _____ repairs all the _____ equipment on the rig.
(electrical/electrician/electricity)

Reading **10** Write the numbers from the CV next to the questions to Anna.

a) What type of business do you work in? _____
b) Where are you working at the moment? _____
c) What's your job title? _____
d) When did you join Omega Studios? _____
e) What qualifications do you have in audio technology? _____
f) Where did you study for your diploma? _____
g) Where did you work before Omega Studios? _____

Speaking **11** Work in pairs, A and B. Take turns to interview each other.

Student A. You are Anna. Answer questions about your CV.

Student B. You are the interviewer. Ask Anna questions about her CV.

Task **12** Write a short version of your CV.

13 Prepare for a job interview. Write notes in answer to these questions about a job you would like to apply for.

- Why do you want this job?
- What skills will you bring to this job?
- Why do you want to leave your present job?
- What questions would you like to ask the interviewers?

14 Work in small groups. Pass your CV around your group. Roleplay a job interview. Take turns to be interviewed by the rest of the group.

1 Match the pictures with the instructions in the box.

> Pull it out.   Push them down.   Pull it forward.   Put it in.   Pull it back.   Pour it in.
> Take it off.   Pick them up.   Switch it on.   Take them out.   Take them away.
> Put it on.   Pour it out.   Switch it off.   Put them down.   Push it in.

2 Complete these dialogues.

1 A: *Have you _switched off_ the engine yet?* (switch off)
   B: No, not yet. I'm _switching it off_ now.
2 A: *Has she _____ the jack yet?* (bring out)
   B: No, she hasn't. Look, she's _____ now.
3 A: *Has he _____ the wheel nuts yet?* (take off)
   B: No, not yet. I think he's _____ at the moment.
4 A: *Have you _____ the new wheels yet?* (put on)
   B: Hold on. I'm _____ right now.
5 A: *Have the mechanics _____ the jacks yet?* (take away)
   B: Not yet, but I think they're _____ now.
6 A: *Has Bill _____ the spark plugs yet?* (put back)
   B: I don't think so. I think he's _____ now.

3 Complete this progress report by the car mechanic (M) to his supervisor (S).

S: *Have you checked the tyres yet?*

M: Yes, we (1) <u>checked</u> (check) all the tyres first thing this morning, and we (2) _____ (find) that the rear OS tyre was worn. So we (3) _____ (replace) it.

S: *What about the tyre pressures? Have you adjusted them yet?*

M: Yes, we (4) _____ (adjust) them when we (5) _____ (put) the tyres on. Then, at about ten this morning, we (6) _____ (examine) the fuel system. We (7) _____ (take) it apart and (8) _____ (unblock) the fuel pipe.

S: *Good. Have you repaired the damaged paintwork on the door?*

M: Yes, we (9) _____ (strip) off the damaged paint just before lunch, and then straight after lunch, we (10) _____ (clean) the door, (11) _____ (repair) it and (12) _____ (repaint) it.

S: *Good. Now what about the air conditioner? Have you checked it?*

M: Yes, we checked it at about three this afternoon. Then we (13) _____ (pump) some new fluid into the air conditioning system.

S: *What about the oil leak under the car? Have you had time to look at that yet?*

M: Yes, we (14) _____ (do) that about an hour ago.

4 Complete these statements with the words in the box.

bring	carry	cover	keep	look	open	press
protect	put	raise	shield	wear		

1 The driver *shields* his eyes from dust by *looking* through the visor on his helmet.

2 The fuel guy _____ the 40 kg fuel hose to the car by _____ it on his shoulders.

3 The wheel jack guys _____ the whole car by _____ jacks under the front and rear.

4 The wheel guys _____ the new tyres warm by _____ them with electric blankets.

5 The mechanics _____ themselves from fire by _____ fire suits.

6 The driver _____ the fuel flap on his car by _____ a button in the cockpit.

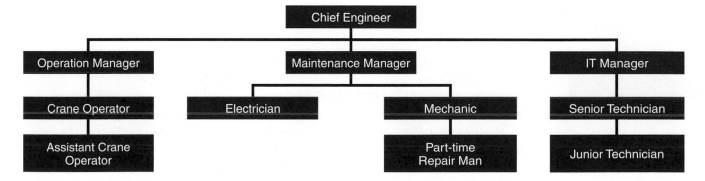

5 Describe the organisation in this department. Use the words in the box.

manage	report to	supervise	work for

6 Complete this job description with the words in the box.

check   have   inspect   make   maintain   order   repair   report   supervise   work

JOB DESCRIPTION OF THE CHIEF MECHANIC ON THE NORD OIL PLATFORM

The Chief Mechanic is responsible for maintaining all the mechanical equipment on the oil rig. He or she
(1) *repairs* the diesel generators, and (2) _____ every machine on the rig. He/She
(3) _____ all the equipment daily, and (4) _____ sure that all machines are in good
working order. He/She (5) _____ broken equipment and (6) _____ replacement parts and
new tools. Most of the time he/she (7) _____ outside or on deck. The Chief Mechanic
(8) _____ to the rig Maintenance Manager, and (9) _____ a small crew of two assistant
mechanics and two motormen. He/She normally (10) _____ a two weeks on/two weeks off schedule.

7 Work in pairs, A and B. Have a phone conversation to arrange a meeting with each other.

Use different structures and verbs: *I'm attending …/I'm going to…/I'm planning to …*

A's plans for next week

● ● ● ● ● ● ● ● ● ● ● ● ● ● ●

MON pm – arrange visit of customers to site
TUE am – go to computer training course
WED pm – show customers around site
THU am – meet new staff

B's plans for next week

● ● ● ● ● ● ● ● ● ● ● ● ● ● ●

MON am – attend project meeting
TUE pm – run training course for staff
WED am – inspect damaged warehouse
THU am – visit trade fair

A: Are you free on Monday morning?
B: No, I'm sorry I'm not. I'm attending a project meeting. How about Monday afternoon?

8 Practise your speed reading. Look for the information you need on the SPEED SEARCH pages (118–119). Try to be the first to complete the task.

Task: Find this advice about job interviews:
- one thing you should do before your interview
- one thing you should do at your interview
- one thing you should not do at your interview

9 Complete this part of a job interview.

- *Where* (1) _____? (you / work)
○ I work at Central Telecoms. I'm a technician there.
- *How long* (2) _____ *there?* (you / be)
○ (3) _____ there for two years. (I / be)
- *And where* (4) _____ *before that?* (you / work)
○ Before that (5) _____ a junior technician at MobileForce. (I / be)
- *Why* (6) _____ *MobileForce?* (you / leave)
○ Because (7) _____ to work in a bigger company. (I / want)
- (8) _____ *your part-time diploma?* (you / finish)
○ Yes, I have.
- *When* (9) _____ *it?* (you / complete)
○ Last July.

10 Identify the devices from their descriptions.

  1 This device sells rail or bus tickets to travellers. The traveller activates it by touching the screen.
  2 This device sounds an alarm when an intruder enters a building. The burglar activates it by interrupting a laser beam.
  3 This machine is located on the rear of a motorboat. The sailor starts it by pulling a handle. The handle is attached to a cord (or cable).
  4 This device makes a motorbike go faster. You activate it by twisting the handle on the handlebars.

11 Correct the mistakes in these sentences.

  1 My brother is a mechanism. He studied mechanical at technique college.
  2 We need to find a good electricity to repair the electrician wires in the house.
  3 I'm a computer technical. How can I help you?
  4 I'm studying for a diploma in electronic. I want to be an electron engineer.

12 Rewrite this email. Replace words/phrases in italics with ones from this list. Make any necessary changes to punctuation.

best wishes; this is to let you know; I'd be grateful if you would; with reference to

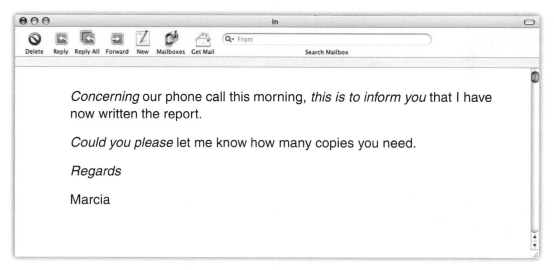

Project **13** Start work on a full version of your own CV.

  • Refer to the Europass template on the Web. (Key *Europass CV* into a search engine).
  • Write a first draft. Remember to update it when your information changes.
  Note: if you have not yet worked in a full-time job, write about part-time or holiday jobs in the Work Experience section of the CV.

14 Research a job you are interested in.

  • Collect interesting job adverts. Make a list of the skills you will need.
  • Find out more about the job.
  • Find out about some companies that you are interested in.
  • Write a description of the job you want.
  • Put all the information you have collected into a special folder.

1 Limits

Start here **1** What do these road signs tell you?

Listening **2** ▶ 🔘 09 A customer wants to drive her car onto a car ferry. Listen to her phone conversation with the sales staff of the ferry company. Complete the specifications of the customer's vehicle on the left.

3 Listen again and complete the conversation.

- How (1) _____ ?
- ○ It's just under (2) _____ metres wide.
- OK, that's fine. The vehicle must not be (3) _____ 2 metres.
- ○ Great.
- (4) _____ ?
- ○ It's exactly (5) _____ metres long.
- Please measure it again carefully. It must not be (6) _____ 7 metres.
- ○ OK, I'll do that and get back to you.
- (7) _____ ?
- ○ It's just over (8) _____ metres high, including the bicycles.
- Mm, that's too high. The vehicle must not be (9) _____ 2.9 metres.
- ○ OK, I'll take the bikes off.

Roof rack

Reading **4** Read the SuperFerries web page. Which vehicles on the left can board the ferry? What are the vehicle types (*large car*, *standard car*, etc.)?

2.9 m
5 m
5 passengers

3.1 m
7.6 m

3.5 m
7 m

1.85 m
5 m
6 passengers

SuperFerries is a cars-only service: we do not take coaches or lorries.

WEIGHT AND DIMENSION LIMITS FOR ALL VEHICLES
Vehicles must not be heavier than 3.5 tonnes. They must not be wider than 2.0 m, longer than 7.0 or higher than 2.9 m.
STANDARD CAR: A 'standard car' must not be longer than 5.0 m, wider than 2.0 m or higher than 1.85 m. It must carry a maximum of five passengers. If it carries more than five persons, it becomes a 'large car'.
LARGE CAR: A 'large car' must not be longer than 7.0 m, wider than 2.0 m or higher than 2.9 m. It must carry no more than nine passengers.
HIGH CAR: A 'high car' must not be higher than 2.9 m, longer than 5.0 m or wider than 2.0 m. It must carry a maximum of five passengers. This vehicle type allows passengers to put extra luggage on the roof of their cars, within the limits.
CAR AND TRAILER: A car and trailer must not be longer than 7.0 m, higher than 2.9 m or wider than 2.0 m. It must carry no more than nine passengers over the age of three.

The comparative form of single-syllable adjectives ends in *-er*, e.g. *longer*, *wider*. Two-syllable adjectives ending in *-y* also end in *-er*, e.g. *noisy* → *noisier*.

Notice the spelling changes: *big* → *bigger*; *wide* → *wider*; *easy* → *easier*.

than is used after the comparative adjective, e.g. *The van is higher than the car.*

Irregular comparatives: *better*, *worse*, *farther/further*, *more* and *less*.

more + adjective is used with adjectives of more than one syllable, e.g. *more expensive*. *less* is used with all types of adjective, e.g. *less cheap*, *less expensive*.

If something is the wrong dimension for something, or above a limit, you can say: *The lorry is too wide for the bridge. The bridge is not wide enough for the lorry.*

5 Explain the problem.

The bridge is 2.7 metres high, but the lorry is 2.9 metres high. The lorry is too high for the bridge.

1 height of bridge: 2.7 m; height of lorry: 2.9 m
2 width of ship: 12.2 m; width of canal: 11.5 m
3 length of plane: 19.3 m; length of hangar: 18.8 m
4 diameter of CD: 12.2 cm; width of box: 11.3 cm
5 thickness of coin: 3 mm; width of slot: 2.88 mm
6 length of screw: 5.5 cm; length of hole: 4.35 cm

Task **6** Work in pairs. Read the text, then discuss the invention. Do you think people will buy it? Give your reasons. Make notes of your discussion.

• compare it with (a) a normal car and (b) a small aircraft
• list (a) its strengths and (b) its weaknesses

The road-ready plane

1 in flying mode

2 in car mode

You can park it in your garage, drive it to your nearest airfield, fly it to your destination, land it, then drive off the runway, along a road to your workplace. In the air, it has a wingspan of 8.4 m, a length of 5.7 m and a height of 2 m. It can fly at a speed of 185 kph for 740 km on a single tank of fuel. The tank holds 76 litres of super-unleaded petrol. In car mode, it can go 17 km per litre of fuel, and can travel at normal car cruising speeds, but it has only two seats and no space for luggage. The cost of the road-ready plane is approximately £75,000.

Writing **7** Work individually. Reply to this email from your company director. Use the notes from your discussion.

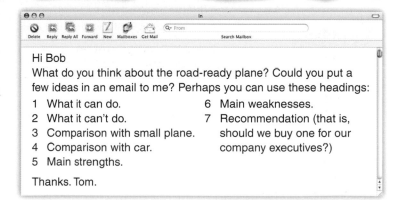

Hi Bob
What do you think about the road-ready plane? Could you put a few ideas in an email to me? Perhaps you can use these headings:

1 What it can do.
2 What it can't do.
3 Comparison with small plane.
4 Comparison with car.
5 Main strengths.
6 Main weaknesses.
7 Recommendation (that is, should we buy one for our company executives?)

Thanks. Tom.

2 Products

Start here

1 Which features are most important to you in a mobile phone? List them in order of importance. Compare your list with your partner's.

Here are some examples: *size of phone, screen size, size of keys, talking time, recharging time, storage capacity, weight, video, music, organised address book.* Think of other features.

Listening

2 ▶ 🔟 Listen and complete the details in the customer call record.

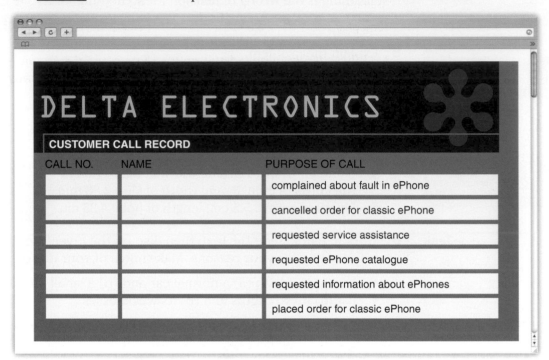

DELTA ELECTRONICS

CUSTOMER CALL RECORD

CALL NO.	NAME	PURPOSE OF CALL
		complained about fault in ePhone
		cancelled order for classic ePhone
		requested service assistance
		requested ePhone catalogue
		requested information about ePhones
		placed order for classic ePhone

3 Listen again and complete the sentences.

1 Sorry, _____ you repeat that, please? (Phone call 1)
2 _____ I have your name, please? (Phone call 2)
3 I _____ like to cancel an order, please. (Phone call 3)
4 _____ you think you _____ tell me the model number, please? (Phone call 3)
5 I _____ like some information about the ePhone, please. (Phone call 4)
6 _____ you like me _____ send you a specification table? (Phone call 4)
7 _____ I put you through to the service department? (Phone call 5)
8 _____ you mind _____ me what the problem is? (Phone call 6)

4 Match the sentences from 3 with these language functions.

a) saying what you want
b) offering to do something
c) asking someone to do something
d) checking information

Speaking

5 Work in pairs. Roleplay phone conversations between customer and service staff. Practise the six dialogues. Use the customer call record in 2.

Study the Audio script on page 121 before you begin.

6 Look at the chart and complete this phone conversation.

Comparison between two ePhones		
	Classic	**Fonarama**
Dimensions	115 x 61 x 11.6 mm	96 x 52 x 9.7 mm
Weight	135 g	94 g
Screen size	88.9 mm (diagonal)	72 mm (diagonal)
Capacity	8GB, 12 GB	8GB, 12GB, 16GB
Battery	16 hours	24 hours
Charging time	3.5 hours	3 hours

A: *What's the difference between the Classic and the Fonarama ePhones?*
B: Well, the Fonarama is much (1) _____ than the Classic. It's only 9.7 mm thick.
A: *I see. And what about the weight?*
B: The Fonarama is much (2) _____ than the Classic. It weighs only 94 g.
A: *OK, and what about the screen size?*
B: The screen of the Fonarama is much (3) _____. It's only 72 mm across.
A: *I prefer a (4) _____ screen size. I want to watch movies on it. I'll order the Classic.*
B: Certainly. Which one would you like? The 8 GB one or the 12 GB one?
A: *The 12 GB one, please.*

7 Practise the conversation. Add more information from the chart.

8 Which word does *one* refer to in this dialogue?

A: *I'd like to buy an MP3 player, please.*
B: Which one would you like? Do you want the white one or the black one?
A: *The black one, please.*

Language *one* is used when someone has already mentioned a thing, there is a choice between two or more types of the thing, and you don't want to repeat the name of the thing.
A: *Please pass me a spanner.*
B: *Which one do you want? The long one or the short one?*

Speaker B wants to mention two types of spanner, but does not want to repeat the word *spanner.*

Speaking **9** The word *one* is missing from four places in this dialogue. Mark the places.

A: Hello, I'd like to buy a portable radio, please.
B: Certainly. We have two colours, red or black. And there are two models. There's with rechargeable batteries, and there's with normal batteries. Which would you like?
A: I'd like the red with the rechargeable batteries, please.

10 ▶ 🔘11 Listen and check your answers.

11 Practise the corrected dialogue with your partner. Use these notes.

Portable radio
model: with rechargeable or normal batteries / **colour**: red or black

3 Equipment

Start here **1** Work in small groups. Discuss these questions about each world record.

- Is it still a world record? If not, what is the new record?
- If it is still a record, how long will it last? Why?

1 The fastest men in the world are Powell and Gatlin. They ran 100 m in 9.77 seconds.
2 The world's tallest building is the Taipei 101 (Taiwan), at 509.2 m.
3 The world's smallest transistor is only 18 nanometres long.
4 The longest stay in space was 437 days by Valeri Polyakov.

Reading **2** Jeff and Bob work in a company that provides motorboats for hire to tourists. Read their email correspondence and answer the questions.

1 What is the purpose of (a) the first email (b) the second email?
2 In the first email, what does Bob (a) remind Jeff about (b) want Jeff to do?
3 In the second email, (a) what new information does Jeff tell Bob (b) what does Jeff promise to do?

Scanning **3** Practise your speed reading. Look for the information you need on the SPEED SEARCH pages (118–119). Try to be the first to complete the task.
Task: Underline the correct answers below.

Specifications
1 Engine A has a (*shorter*/*longer*) shaft than Engine B.
2 The heaviest engine is Engine (*A*/*B*/*C*/*D*/*E*).
3 Engine D is the (*cheapest*/*most expensive*) engine.
4 Engine C is (*as powerful as*/*more powerful than*/*less powerful than*) Engine E.

Test results
1 The (*fastest*/*slowest*) engine was Engine C.
2 The (*most rapid*/*least rapid*) acceleration from 0–40 km/h was Engine C.
3 The (*quietest*/*noisiest*) engine was Engine B.
4 The engine with the lowest fuel consumption was Engine (*A*/*B*/*C*/*D*/*E*).

Language To change the comparative into the superlative form, change *-er* to *-est*, *more* to *most* and *less* to *least*, e.g. *longest, widest, biggest, noisiest, most expensive, least noisy*.

the is used in front of the superlative, e.g. *the fastest car in the world*.

There are five irregular superlatives: *best, worst, farthest/furthest, most* and *least*.

Speaking **4** Make comparisons. Think of as many differences as possible. Think of some more groups and make comparisons.

1 Zinedine Zidane / Wayne Rooney / Cristiano Ronaldo
2 Mount Everest / North Face of the Eiger / Aconcagua
3 coal-fired power / nuclear power / wind power
4 diesel / petrol / LPG

5 Work in pairs. Write down three items or products you know about. Compare them and make notes.

Task **6** Work in small groups. Have a meeting to discuss this problem and agree on the best solution.

4 x 4 = four wheel drive
say: *four by four*

You and the other members of your group work on an oil rig in a desert. The rig is about 130 km from the nearest town. The town has a small airport. There is no road between the town and the rig, and an aircraft cannot land at the rig. Between the town and the rig the land is sandy and rocky, with some hills. Your team needs to transport small teams of three to eight engineers and to tow a trailer with heavy drilling equipment between the airport and the rig. Your team wants to buy a 4x4 with the following features:

- long wheelbase
- high clearance
- powerful engine
- space for up to 8 passengers
- low fuel consumption
- large fuel tank
- towing power (able to pull other vehicles)
- high cab (to allow driver to see easily)
- low price

Student A: your information is on page 111.
Student B: your information is on page 113.
Student C: your information is on page 115.
Student D: your information is on page 117.

Writing **7** Work individually. Write a short report on your meeting. Give your group's decision and the reasons for the decision. Use these headings.

1 Introduction
Our team held a meeting yesterday to choose …

2 Comparison of four vehicles
We compared the specifications of the four vehicles:
1.1 The Toyota Land Cruiser has the longest wheelbase. It is 2850 mm in length.
1.2 …

3 Decision
We decided to buy the _____ because …

Processes

1 Infrastructure

drill	
cutter face	
conveyor belt	
teeth	
leg	shoe

Start here **1** What is this? What does it do? How does it work? Discuss with your partner.

Listening **2** 🔊 12 Listen and complete the specifications chart.

Reading **3** Read this article and put these headings in the correct place.

Collecting the rocks Controlling the movement Moving the cutter
Cutting the rock surface Strengthening the roof Supplying the electricity

MB471/316 Tunnel Drill Specifications	
Length	
Diameter	
Speed	
Manpower needed	
Cost	

THE MB471-316 TUNNEL DRILL – one of the largest hard-rock drills in the world

1 _____

The face of the cutter has 85 teeth. Each tooth is 60 cm long. The cutter face rotates about seven times a minute. When it rotates, the teeth cut large circles into the surface of the rock.

2 _____

Pieces of rock fall to the ground. They are collected by large scoops. They are then dropped into chutes. When the cutter face rotates upwards, the rocks fall onto conveyor belts. They are then carried to the rear of the machine.

3 _____

Hydraulic cylinders push the body of the cutter slowly forwards. As it moves forwards, steel shoes move outwards and grip the tunnel walls. At the same time, two legs push down and lift the machine off the floor.

4 _____

Fifteen electric motors supply the machine with 6,375 horsepower. The power is connected to the cutters by means of a 13,800-volt cable.

5 _____

There are two drills attached to steel arms. These are located immediately behind the cutters. When the machine moves forwards, holes are drilled into the roof of the tunnel. Then the holes are filled with bolts and cement. This strengthens the roof.

6 _____

The machine operator sits in a cabin at the heart of the machine. Here he/she controls its speed and direction. Video cameras monitor the cutter and the tunnel.

Vocabulary **4** Make a list of all the names of parts of the body and clothing in the text in 3.

5 List other technical contexts where the items in 4 are used.

Example: 'teeth' are also found on gears.

Language In an active sentence, the subject = the agent. The subject does the action.

Subject = agent	Active verb	Object
Hydraulic cylinders	push	the cutter.
Large scoops	collect	the rocks.

In a passive sentence, the subject is NOT the same as the agent. The subject does not do the action. The agent does the action to the subject.

Subject	Passive verb		Agent
	be	Past participle	
The cutter	is	pushed	by hydraulic cylinders.
The rocks	are	collected	by large scoops.

6 Change this set of instructions into a description of a process, using the passive and the words in the box.

> finally   first   next   now   then

How to change the oil in a car

1	Run the engine for a few minutes.	5	Put the oil drain plug on
2	Switch off the engine.	6	Take off the oil filler cap.
3	Take off the oil drain plug.	7	Pour in the new oil.
4	Empty the old oil into a container.	8	Put the oil filler cap back on.

Begin: First the engine is run for a few minutes. Then it is switched off. Now the …

7 Make a set of instructions about a process you know about. Then rewrite it as a process description in the passive.

Examples of processes: food manufacture, steel making, canning, assembling computer components, manufacturing a CD, dairy processing.

8 Fill in the gaps, using the correct form of the verbs in brackets.

1 Large drills _____ (make) holes in the roof of the tunnel. Then the holes _____ (fill) with bolts and cement.
2 A large propeller _____ (push) the hovercraft forwards. The propeller _____ (drive) by a powerful engine.
3 Hot water _____ (flow) from the engine into the radiator. Here it _____ (cool) by the fan.
4 The robot _____ (monitor) by a computer. This computer also _____ (control) all the other robots in the building.
5 First, the rusty machine parts _____ (bring) into the factory. Then they _____ (clean). Then the rust _____ (remove). Next the parts _____ (paint). Finally, they _____ (take) out of the factory again.

9 Make a list of headings for the main stages of a process you know about. Make each heading begin with a verb ending in **-ing**, like the ones in 3.

Example: Moulding and shaping steel – 1 Melting the steel; 2 Casting; 3 Cooling; 4 Rolling the steel; 5 Straightening; 6 Cutting.

10 Give a short talk to the class explaining your process. Use your headings.

2 Manufacturing

Start here **1** What do you know about cars? Discuss with a partner the location and function of these parts: *body, chassis, drive shaft, axle, transmission.*

2 The photos show the main stages in assembling a car, but they are in the wrong order. Write the figure numbers in the correct boxes in the flow chart.

3 Make captions for the six photos with the verbs and nouns in the box. Use verbs ending in *-ing*.

> add   attach   install   paint   test   weld   body   chassis   finished car   parts

Example: Fig 6. Welding the body panels to the body frame.

Reading   **4**   Read this website of a car company and check your answers to 2 and 3.

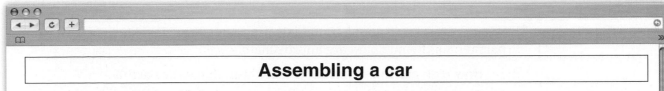

Assembling a car

First, the parts are delivered by truck or rail to the *delivery area* of the car assembly plant. From here, some parts are taken to the body shop, and other parts are transported to the chassis line. The parts are carried around the plant by forklift trucks or conveyor belts.

In the *body shop*, the panels are welded to the frame to form the body of the car. This is done by more than 400 robots.

Then the body is taken to the *paint shop*. Here it is cleaned and painted by robots. Special clothing is worn by the robots to protect the paint. After this, the body is checked by human workers to look for faults.

Next, the painted body moves along a conveyor belt to the *trim line* and many parts are added to it. For example, the instrument panel, the air conditioning system, the heating system and the electrical wiring are all installed here. The windscreen is inserted by robots using laser guides.

Meanwhile, in the *chassis line*, components are added to the chassis. First, the chassis is turned upside down, to make the work easier. Then the fuel system, the transmission, the suspension, the exhaust system, the axles and the drive shaft are all installed. Next the chassis is turned over (rightside up). The engine is lowered into the chassis and connected to it.

Now the chassis and the body move simultaneously to the *final assembly line*. Here the body is attached to the chassis, and all the final parts are added. The tyres and the radiator are added here. The hoses are connected, and the radiator and air conditioner are filled with fluid. The car's central computer is also installed here.

Lastly, the finished car and all electrical systems are tested. The car is filled with fuel and the engine is started for the first time. The car is put on special rollers to test the engine and the wheels. If it passes the test, the car is finally driven out of the assembly plant.

Language   *to* + verb is used to talk or write about the purpose of an action.

Why do you paint the car body? To protect it from rust.
The car body is painted to protect it from rust.

Speaking   **5**   Match actions with their purposes. Refer to the text in 4.

	action		purpose of action
1	workers weld thin metal sheets to a frame	a)	to check the movement of the wheels
2	they turn the chassis upside down	b)	to make the car body
3	the robots wear special clothes	c)	to inspect it for faults in the paint
4	they turn the chassis rightside up	d)	to protect the wet paint from dust
5	workers put the finished car on rollers	e)	to install the fuel system easily
6	workers check the car body by hand	f)	to lower the engine into it

6   In pairs, ask and answer the questions in 5. Use the passive form in the question.

A: *Why are thin metal sheets welded to a frame?*
B: *To make the car body.*

7   Ask questions to get these answers. Refer to the text in 4.

1   They're delivered by truck or rail.
2   They're welded together in the body shop.
3   They're carried by forklift trucks or conveyor belts.
4   To look for faults in the paint.
5   It's done by human workers.
6   It's done using laser guides.

3 Communications

Start here **1** What do you know about communications satellites? Do this quiz with your partner. All the numbers are approximate.

1 How high are communications satellites above the Earth?
  a) 15,000 km   b) 25,000 km   c) 35,000 km   d) 45,000 km
2 How fast do these satellites travel around the Earth?
  a) 7000 km/h   b) 11,000 km/h   c) 15,000 km/h   d) 21,000 km/h
3 What frequency are signals from a communications satellite to your satellite dish?
  a) 12 GHz   b) 1 GHz   c) 500,000 MHz   d) 5000 MHz
4 What frequency are the signals from your satellite dish to your TV?
  a) 150 MHz   b) 1500 MHz   c) 15,000 MHz   d) 150,000 MHz

Scanning **2** Practise your speed reading. Look for the information you need on the SPEED SEARCH pages (118–119). Try to be the first to complete this task.

Task: Check your answers to the quiz in 1.

Reading **3** Read this instruction leaflet and label the diagram with the words in the box.

computer   dish   DTV card   feed horn   satellite   TV   TV station

Transmitting   Receiving

How to receive satellite digital video broadcasts

Equipment needed

You will need a computer with a DTV (digital TV) card.
5 This is connected by cable to a satellite dish, which should be between 60 cm and 1.8 m in diameter. The dish must have a feed horn. This converts high-frequency signals to low-frequency ones.

10 How it works

There is a communications satellite in orbit high above the Earth. TV programmes are transmitted from TV stations up to the satellite, which then sends the signals down to Earth. These signals have a high frequency of 15 several GHz.
Your dish receives the high-frequency signals and reflects them to the feed horn, which then converts the signal into a lower frequency.
The feed horn is connected via a cable to the DTV card, 20 which processes the signal. It extracts the video and audio, and plays them via the PC monitor and speakers.

4 What does *which* refer to in the text?

via = by means of

1 line 5   a) the cable   b) the satellite dish
2 line 13   a) the satellite   b) the TV stations
3 line 17   a) the frequency   b) the feed horn
4 line 20   a) the DTV card   b) the feed horn

| Signals are transmitted to | the satellite. The satellite | then sends the signals to Earth. |
| | the satellite, which | |

| John reports to | Adel. Adel | is the training manager. |
| | Adel, who | |

5 Join these pairs of sentences. Use *who* or *which*.

1 My computer has a DTV card. This is connected by cable to my satellite dish.
2 If your DTV card doesn't work, contact our technician. He will repair it.
3 The dish reflects the signal to the feed horn. This converts the signal to a lower frequency.
4 Please send any complaints to our customer service manager. She will then contact you.
5 The radio station sends signals to the satellite. This then transmits the signals to my dish.
6 My DTV card extracts the audio and video. These are then displayed on my PC monitor.

Example: 1 My computer has a DTV card, which is connected by cable to my satellite dish.

Vocabulary **6** Match words with the same or similar meaning.

| transmit receive convert | get send take out |
| extract display operate | change work show |

7 Complete the sentences. Notice the hyphens (-).

1 The signal has a high frequency. It's a *high-frequency* signal.
2 This pump uses high pressure. It's a _____ pump.
3 The fuse breaks at 13 amps. It's a *13-amp* fuse. (Note: amps → amp)
4 The cable carries 13,800 volts. It's a _____ cable.
5 My satellite dish is 1.8 metres wide. It's a _____ dish.

Speaking **8** Draw a simple diagram and make notes about a setup you know about. If you prefer, use this satellite dish setup and make notes about the diagram.

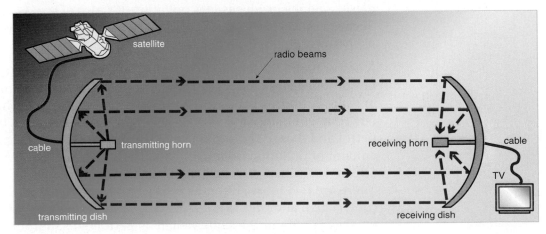

9 Describe the setup and explain to the class how it works.

1 Choose two of these cars and make comparisons between them.

Car 1: the Audi TT 2.0T FSI	
Fuel tank capacity	55 L
Engine size	1,984 cc
Top speed	149 mph
Acceleration	0 to 62 mph: 6.6 sec.
Fuel consumption	36.7 mpg
CO_2 emission	183 g/km

Car 2: the BMW Z4 2.0i SE Roadster	
Fuel tank capacity	55 L
Engine size	1,998 cc
Top speed	137 mph
Acceleration	0 to 62 mph: 8.2 sec.
Fuel consumption	37.7 mpg
CO_2 emission	181 g/km

Car 3: the Saab 93 convertible 1.8t 150bhp	
Fuel tank capacity	62 L
Engine size	1,998 cc
Top speed	127 mph
Acceleration	0 to 60 mph: 11.0 sec.
Fuel consumption	37.2 mpg
CO_2 emission	233 g/km

2 Compare all three cars. Say which one you like best, and why.

3 Complete the text.

Which is the better fuel for a car? Is it petrol or diesel? Petrol is (1) _more common_ (common) because it makes a car go (2) _faster_ (fast) than diesel. It's also much (3) _less noisy_ (noisy) than diesel. Diesel usually costs less than petrol, and you can travel for more kilometres per litre, because diesel has about 10% more energy per litre than petrol. But diesel engines are (4) _____ (noisy) and (5) _____ (heavy) than petrol ones, although they last longer. From an environmental point of view, diesel oil is (6) _____ (good) than petrol, because the exhaust from diesel engines produces less pollution. It's also (7) _____ (safe). Because diesel is (8) _____ (combustible) than petrol, it's less likely to catch fire in an accident.

A newer fuel, LPG (Liquid Petroleum Gas), makes cars go as fast as petrol, but produces less energy per litre. However, LPG is becoming very popular in some countries because it's the (9) _____ (harmful) to the environment compared with diesel or petrol. Of the three types of fuel (LPG, petrol and diesel), cars that use LPG emit the (10) _____ (small) amount of pollution from their exhaust. LPG is also the (11) _____ (clean) fuel when you're filling the car, because the gas is completely sealed. There are two more strengths of LPG: it's the (12) _____ (quiet) fuel, and the (13) _____ (expensive) of the three. LPG engines are about the same weight as petrol ones, but they're much (14) _____ (durable).

4 Match the sentences with their language functions.

Sentence		Language function
1	I'm sorry about the delay.	a) saying what you want
2	Sorry, could you repeat your surname, please?	b) offering to do something
3	Is that B-E-N or B-E-N-N?	c) checking what someone said
4	Would you mind sending me the invoice today?	d) asking someone to do something
5	I'd like to speak to the manager, please.	e) checking how to spell something
6	Would you like mc to send you a brochure?	f) apologising for doing something

5 Complete the phone conversation. Add capital letters where necessary. You don't need all the words in the box.

I	I'll	I'd	do	did	will	shall	would	could

● *MobileExpress. This is Customer Service, Robert speaking. How can I help you?*

○ Hello. (1) _____ like some information about your new mobile phone, please.

● *Certainly. (2) _____ you like me to send you a brochure?*

○ Yes, please. Do you think you (3) _____ send it by email?

● *Of course. (4) _____ I send it as a Word attachment?*

○ Yes, that's fine.

● *Good. So (5) _____ I have your email address, please?*

○ Yes, it's db30@easisoft.com

● *Sorry, (6) _____ you say db13?*

○ No, db30.

● *Thanks. And how (7) _____ you spell easisoft?*

○ E-A-S-I-S-O-F-T.

● *Right. (8) _____ send it today.*

6 The word *one* is missing from six places in this dialogue. Mark the places.

● *Hello, I'd like to buy an external hard drive, please.*

○ Certainly. We have two types. There's with a cable, and there's a wireless. And there are two types of cable. There's with a USB connection, and there's with FireWire connection. Which would you like?

● *I'd like the with the USB cable connection, please.*

7 Match these descriptions of a 4 x 4 vehicle.

1	it has a long wheelbase	a)	it can drive a long way on one tank of petrol
2	it has low fuel consumption	b)	it can pull another vehicle or trailer easily
3	it has high clearance	c)	the petrol tank is very big
4	it has strong towing power	d)	the drive shaft is long
5	it has large fuel capacity	e)	the driver can see clearly all around
6	it has good driver visibility	f)	there's a lot of space between the ground and the chassis

8 Change these instructions into a description of a process, using the passive.

How to clean a spark plug

1 Take off the spark plug cover.
2 Loosen the spark plug with a special wrench.
3 Remove the spark plug from the socket.
4 Clean the spark plug using a wire brush.
5 Replace the spark plug in the socket.
6 Tighten the spark plug using the wrench.
7 Put the cover back on the spark plug.

Begin: First of all, the spark plug cover is taken off.
Then the spark plug is ...

9 Change the second paragraph into a set of instructions, using imperatives.

You can make your own radio using a few simple components: two lengths of wire (one 3 m long, and the other 6 m long), a metal rod, earphones and a detector. This is how to do it.

First, the rod is hammered into the ground. Then the insulation is stripped off the end of the 3-metre wire. The wire is twisted around the rod ten times to make a good connection. This is the earth wire. Next, the detector is attached to the other end of the earth wire. The 6-metre wire is now taken and one end is connected to the other end of the detector. (This wire is your antenna.) The antenna is hung from a tree (making sure that the bare end does not touch the earth). The two wires from the earphones are connected to each end of the detector. Finally, the earphones are put on. Now you can hear the radio station (if you are very close to the transmitter!).

Begin: 1 Hammer the rod into the ground.
2 Strip the insulation off the end of the 3-metre wire.

10 Make a set of headings for a talk on these topics. Make each heading begin with a verb ending in **-ing**.

1 First, I'd like to talk about how the communications satellite is launched.
2 After that, I'll talk about how the programmes are transmitted to the satellite.
3 Then I'll look at how the digital signals are received from the satellite.
4 Next, I'll explain how your satellite dish and digital receiver are installed.
5 Then I'll go on to mention how your dish is connected to the digital TV receiver.
6 The next topic is how high-frequency signals are converted to low-frequency ones.
7 And then I'll move on to how the video and audio are extracted from the digital signal.
8 Finally, I'll mention how the video and audio are played via the monitor and speakers.
Example: 1 Launching the communications satellite

11 Complete these. Use hyphens (-). Note: Be careful with plural nouns.

1 The plane is ready for the road. It's a _road-ready_ plane.
2 The engine has a cycle of four strokes. It's a _4-stroke_ engine.
3 The propeller has three blades. It's a _____ propeller.
4 The cable is six metres long. It's a _____ cable.
5 This computer is activated when you use your voice. It's a _____ computer.
6 That ticket machine starts when you touch the screen. It's a _____ ticket machine.

12 Ask and answer questions about a car assembly plant.

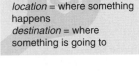

location = where something happens
destination = where something is going to

Action	Purpose, method, agent, time, location, destination
1 deliver car parts	a) _method_: truck or rail
	b) _destination_: delivery area
2 carry parts	a) _destination_: different parts of plant
	b) _method_: forklift trucks or conveyor belts
3 weld panels to frame	a) _location_: body shop
	b) _agent_: 400 robots
	c) _purpose_: make the body of car
4 check the car body	a) _time_: after painting
	b) _agent_: human workers
	c) _purpose_: look for faults in the paint
5 insert windscreen	a) _destination_: front of car body
	b) _agent_: robots
	c) _method_: laser guides
6 move chassis and body simultaneously	a) _destination_: final assembly line
	b) _purpose_: attach body to chassis

1 a) _How are the car parts delivered? They're delivered by truck or rail._
  b) _Where are they delivered? To the delivery area._

13 Write full sentences using the passive.

Example: 1 The car parts are delivered to the delivery area by truck or rail.

14 Rewrite this set of instructions as a paragraph describing a process. Use the passive form of the verbs.

Servicing a car battery

Open the bonnet of the car. Locate the battery.
Loosen the battery cables, using a wrench. Remove the battery cables from the posts.
Always remove the negative (or earth) cable first, then the positive.
Carefully lay the detached ends of the cables to one side.
Wipe away corrosion from the top of the battery, using baking soda and water.
If corrosion is very heavy, you can clean it from the posts using a wire brush.
Apply petroleum jelly to the inside of the terminals and the posts.
Reattach the cables. Close the car bonnet.

Begin: First the bonnet of the car is opened and the battery is located. Then ...

Project 15 Research an industry you are interested in.

- Find out about an important process in the industry.
- Draw a flow chart of the main stages in the process.
- Write a description of the process.
- Explain the process to the class.

Descriptions

1 Uses

Start here

1 Think of some tools or devices you use. Discuss why they are useful with a partner.

Reading

2 Read these advertisements and match the objects with their descriptions.

1 Use the X-beam wrench for loosening tight and rusty old bolts without hurting your hand. The ends are at ninety degrees to each other, so you always grip a wide, flat surface, not a narrow edge.

2 What do you do if your car battery goes flat in a storm, and you don't have jump leads or roadside assistance? The Black & Decker Simple Start allows you to start your car without getting wet. It plugs into the 12-volt socket in your car, and it's designed to restart your car in ten minutes.

3 This is designed to jump, dive, roll and move over and under water at 30 mph using a 175-hp engine. Innespace Sea Breacher is a two-seat, 5-metre long, underwater vehicle, shaped like a dolphin. It acts as a jetski and as a fast submarine.

4 Have you forgotten where you put your keys? Use this smart device to find them. Simply attach the electronic tag to your keys. Then, if you can't find them later, switch on Loc8tor, and it will point in the right direction – not only left or right, but up or down too. It will show you where your keys are. At the same time, the tag on your keys will emit a beeping sound.

Speaking

3 Discuss the objects in 2 with a partner. What do you think of them? Are they useful for you?

Listening

4 ▶ 🔘13 Listen to these inventors answering questions about their inventions. Identify the inventions.

    a) Invention number _____
    b) Invention number _____
    c) Invention number _____

5 Listen again and complete the dialogues.

    A: So, tell me about your invention. What's it for?
    B: It's (1) _____ .
    A: OK. And what about this device. What's it used for?
    B: It's (2) _____ .
    A: Tell me about this invention. What can it be used for?
    B: You (3) _____ .

Present simple	What does the carburettor do? It mixes air and petrol.
for + verb -ing	What's this tool for? It's for hammering in nails. What's this machine used for? It's used for producing drinking water.
to + verb	You use this machine to charge batteries. This device is designed to find lost objects.
act as + noun	The fan of a hovercraft acts as a propeller.

Speaking

6 Work in pairs. Make questions and answers about the uses of the devices in 2.

A: *What's this device used for?*
B: *It's used for turning nuts and bolts without hurting your hand.*

7 What do you think these devices are used for? Discuss them with your partner.

Vocabulary

Many nouns end in *-er* or *-or*. These are often *agent nouns*. An agent noun shows the person or thing that does an action, e.g. A *calculator* (n.) is a machine. It *calculates* (vb.) sums.
Note these changes of spelling when you add *-er/-or*:
- double the final consonant after a short vowel. *Example: propel → propeller*
- delete the final *-e*. *Example: receive → receiver*

8 Find the agent nouns for the verbs in the box. Use a dictionary if necessary.

> calculate   conduct   contain   generate   receive   stabilise   transmit

9 Fill in the blanks. Use nouns from the list in 8.

1 The number pad on a computer can be used as a _____ .
2 Your body can act as a _____ of electricity in a thunderstorm.
3 A car engine functions as a _____ when it recharges the battery.
4 The antenna on a mobile phone operates as a _____ and as a _____ of radio signals.

Task

10 Work in small groups. Choose one of these objects with your group.

a tin can, a belt, a brick, a tyre, a water pipe

- brainstorm as many unusual uses for them as you can
- write down your best ideas
- present your group's best ideas to the class

Examples: **A tin can** – *You can use it to store pencils. You can put flowers in it. You can use it as a cup. Two or three cans together can act as a door bell,* etc.

2 Appearance

Start here **1** Do you know where these buildings are?

(Answers on page 115)

2 Choose one of the buildings. Don't tell your partner which one. Describe its appearance. Can your partner identify it from your description?

Reading **3** Read these newspaper cuttings. Match the descriptions with the buildings.

1 This building looks like a huge ship, an ocean liner, sailing up the river. One part of the building is shaped like three hulls. The other part looks like the decks and the bridge.

2 The building looks like a TV transmitter. It has three spherical structures. The bottom two are connected by a structure which is shaped like a ladder. It looks like three onions on a skewer! The foot of the building has legs, like a tripod.

3 It's triangular at the base, but thin and rectangular at the top. It looks like a huge chisel, with an empty space in the middle of the blade.

4 The skyscraper is shaped like a giant sail. The sail is standing on a short surfboard in the sea.

5 This building is in three parts. In the centre there's a tall H-shaped building. On the left there's the top part of a dome. It looks like an upside-down plate. On the right there's the bottom part of a dome, like a soup bowl.

6 It consists of three L-shaped structures, attached to each other. It looks like a square link in a chain.

Language You can describe the *shape* or *appearance* of something in these ways:

- *The building **looks like** a TV transmitter.*
- *The building **is shaped like** a dome. It's a dome-**shaped** building.*
- *The plan is **in the shape of** an L. It's an L-**shaped** plan.*
- *The screen is **in the shape of a circle**. It's a **circular** screen.*

4 Describe the buildings in the photos in 2. Cover up the texts in 3.

Vocabulary

5 Match the nouns to the shapes.

circle cone cube cylinder hemisphere rectangle
semicircle sphere square triangle

6 Write an adjective for each noun.

Example: cylinder – cylindrical

7 Underline the stressed syllable in each word.

| 1 | tri ang le | 3 | cir cu lar | 5 | tri ang u lar | 7 | rect ang le |
| 2 | rect ang u lar | 4 | cy lin der | 6 | circ le | 8 | cy lind ric al |

8 ▶ 🔊 14 Listen and check your answers to 7.

9 Underline the correct words.

1 A surfboard sail is roughly *triangle/triangular* in shape, with one curved side.
2 A food tin (or can) is basically a metal *cylinder/cylindrical*.
3 TVs and computers normally have *rectangle/rectangular* screens.
4 Don't cut that wood with the hand saw. It's quicker to use the *circle/circular* saw.
5 My bass amplifier is the new *cube/cubic* model. It's exactly 30 x 30 x 30 cm.
6 The Earth is not a perfect *sphere/spherical*. It is flatter at the poles.
7 The spaceship's re-entry capsule is in the shape of a *cone/conical*.
8 A protractor is a *semi-circle/semi-circular* instrument for measuring angles.

10 Match the names of the objects in the box with their pictures.

A-frame E-clip G-clamp G-clip T-junction U-bend U-bolt V-engine

Task

11 Work in pairs, A and B. Play ***twenty questions***.

Student A: Think of an everyday object. It could be a vehicle, a tool, a measuring instrument or a useful device. Don't tell your partner what it is. Answer your partner's questions.

Student B: Ask a maximum of 20 questions and try to guess Student A's object. You can't ask directly *What is it?* But you can ask questions like these:

- **appearance:** *What does it look like? What colour is it? What shape is it?*
- **use:** *What's it for? What's it used for? What does it do?*
- **materials:** *What's it made of?*
- **dimensions:** *How long is it? How wide is it?*
- **properties:** *Is it flexible? Is it water-resistant?*

When you have finished, change roles.

3 Definitions

Start here **1** Here are some ideas for devices that appeared on a TV programme for inventors and entrepreneurs. Which ideas do you think were successful? Discuss with a partner.

(Answers on page 113)

- **Are you a technical entrepreneur?**
- **Do you have a good idea for inventing and manufacturing a new device?**
- **Do you think you can sell your device and make a profit?**
- **Do you need money to start your business?**

Explain your idea to a team of rich business experts – the Dragons. Try to persuade them to invest their money in your idea. Here are some ideas from previous programmes:

1   An electronic device for boiling eggs without using water.
2   A boat alarm system for finding an MOB (man overboard).
3   A music website for downloading and mixing dance music.
4   A seat belt adjuster for protecting children in car booster seats.

Listening **2** ▶ 🎧 **15** The four inventors in 1 are making their opening statements. Listen and complete the sentences with *which*, *who* or *that*.

1   My invention is an electronic device (1) _____ can boil eggs without using water.
2   LifeGuard is an alarm system (2) _____ can find someone (3) _____ has fallen off a boat.
3   This is a music website (4) _____ allows you to download and mix dance music.
4   It's a seat belt adjuster (5) _____ protects children in car booster seats.

Language

Word	*be*	Type	Defining relative clause	
			Pronoun	Function
LifeGuard	is	an alarm system	which	can find an MOB.
MusicWorld	is	a website	that	downloads dance music.
Inventors	are	people	who	create new devices.

- *which* is used with things
- *who* is used with people
- *that* can replace *which* or *who*

3 Fill in the blanks with the most suitable 'type' noun in the box.

| device | instrument | system | technician | tool | vehicle |

1 A solar panel is a/an _____. It converts sunlight into electricity.
2 The hovercraft is a/an _____. It carries people over land and sea.
3 A lab assistant is a/an _____. He or she maintains the equipment in a laboratory.
4 A torque wrench is a/an _____. It tightens nuts and bolts.
5 GPS is a satellite _____. It gives the location of objects on the ground.
6 An ammeter is a/an _____. It measures electric current.

4 Combine each pair of sentences in 3 into a single sentence in the form of a definition. Use *which*, *who* or *that*.

Example: 1 A solar panel is a device which converts sunlight into electricity.

5 Read this advertisement and answer the questions below.

Alarm pods

Hydrophone

Display

This digital-sonar alarm system transmits a signal to your boat crew if you fall overboard into the water. It consists of three devices: the alarm pod, the hydrophone and the display.

The alarm pod is an egg-shaped device, worn by each crew member, which transmits a digital-sonar coded signal when it is submerged in water.

The hydrophone is a transducer, attached to the inside of the boat hull, that listens for signals from the alarm pod.

The display is a control unit, attached to the dashboard of the boat, which shows information from the hydrophone by means of LEDs and digital displays.

When the MOB (man overboard) hits the water, the alarm pod is submerged. The alarm pod has two pins. If these pins are in contact with water for one second, and the contact is constant across the two pins, the pod is activated. It then sends a signal under the water. This signal is picked up by the hydrophone, which relays it to the display.

Four things then happen immediately:
- Bright LEDs in the display show a visible alarm.
- Speakers on the boat sound an audible alarm.
- The MOB's location is shown on the display via the internal GPS system.
- Red and green LEDs navigate the boat to the MOB's location.

1 Which device acts as (a) the transmitter (b) the receiver (c) the controller?
2 Which device is fixed (a) inside the hull (b) on the crew's body (c) on the deck?
3 What happens if drops of rain fall on the pins on the alarm pod? Does the alarm sound? Why/Why not?
4 Does the signal travel from the pod to the display unit (a) directly (b) via the hydrophone (c) via GPS (satellite)?
5 Which word in the text means (a) able to be seen (b) able to be heard?

6 Work in small groups. Decide on an idea for a new invention. In a single sentence, give the definition of your device. Then, in a few sentences, explain how it works.

1 Safety

Start here **1** Make a list of the hazards (A-H) in this warehouse in note form.

shelf

A

B

C

D

fork

forklift truck

aisle

pallet

ramp

E

F

G

H

hand truck

Reading **2** Read this warehouse safety poster. Match the rules to the hazards in 1.

Warehouse safety
1 Hand trucks must not be overloaded.
2 Aisles have to be kept free of all blockages.
3 Boxes need to be pushed in until they are level with the edge of the shelf.
4 Gas cylinders must always be strapped or chained to hand trucks.
5 The forks of a forklift truck must never be used for carrying people.
6 Larger boxes should not be stacked on higher shelves.
7 Trucks must be pulled, not pushed, up a ramp.
8 Only one item should be removed from a shelf at one time.

Language

Helmets	must/should/have to/need to		be	worn here.
	must/should	not		taken off.

3 Where can you see these labels? What do they mean?

4 What could be inside containers with the labels?

bottles of liquid   fruit   food   glass   hats   electrical goods   plants

5 Complete these explanations of the labels. Use the correct form of the modals and the passive form of the verbs in brackets.

1   This item _____ (need / handle) carefully.
It _____ (must not / drop or throw).

2   This item _____ (need / carry) this way up.
It _____ (must not / turn) upside down.

3   This item _____ (should / keep) inside the warehouse.
It _____ (have / protect) from the rain.

4   This box _____ (should / deliver) as soon as possible.
It _____ (must not / leave) for more than three days.

5   This box _____ (have / freeze).
It _____ (must not / leave) outside the freezer.

Example: 1 This item needs to be handled carefully. It must not be …

6 Change the instructions in 5 into the active form.

Example: 1 You need to handle this item carefully. You mustn't …

Task   7 Three safety procedures have become mixed up. Work in pairs, A and B. Put all the notes together under the best headings in the best order. Each procedure has eight steps.

Student A: turn to page 112 to find your set of notes.
Student B: use the notes below.

CPR

FIRST AID AFTER
ELECTRIC SHOCK

CHEMICAL SPILL
PROCEDURE

FIRE EVACUATION
PROCEDURE

If you hear an alarm, remain calm.

Do not return to the building unless you are authorised by the fire department.

Check the person's condition.

If there is no pulse, give the person CPR.

If the person is breathing, they should be placed in the recovery position.

Do not stop to collect your belongings.

Remain near workroom until Chemical Safety staff arrives.

Stop work.

The workroom must be secured to keep others out.

Move at least 30 metres from building.

Attend to any injured persons if you can do so safely.

Call 112.

Recovery position

Artificial
respiration

2 Emergency

Start here

1 Work in small groups. Decide on a plan to rescue the diver.

> Mike and Ben are scuba divers. They go in their motorboat about 2 km from land and drop anchor. Mike dives down to a shipwreck on the seabed. Ben stays on the boat. Mike has an accident, and injures his leg. His leg is trapped in the shipwreck and he can't move. After some time, Ben knows that Mike has a problem. He dives to look for Mike.

In your group,
- brainstorm and make a list of all the tasks Ben has to do, in any order
- discuss and decide on the best order to do the tasks

Listening

2 ▶ 💿 16 Listen to this diving instructor brainstorming with trainees how to rescue someone trapped under water. Number the points in the order in which they are mentioned.

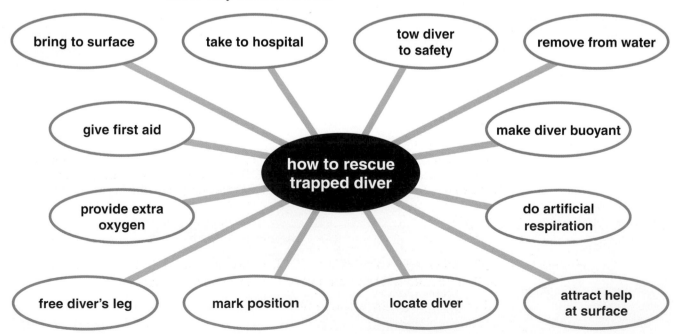

3 🔊 **17** Now the instructor is getting the trainees to put their ideas into the best order. Listen and number these notes in the correct order.

- Diver's oxygen low? → Give extra gas cylinder to diver.
- Diver's location under water unknown? → Locate diver and mark their position. _1_
- Diver not buoyant at the surface? → Inflate diver's wet suit.
- Not breathing? → Give artificial respiration.
- Other boats in area? → Send signal for help.
- Serious injury? → Call helicopter to take to hospital.
- Diver close to boat or land? → Remove from water.
- No help available at surface? → Tow diver to boat or land.
- Diver trapped underwater? → Free diver with knife.
- Diver submerged in water? → Bring to surface carefully.
- Diver needs immediate treatment? → Give first aid.

they is often used to mean
he or she
them is often used to mean
him or her
their is often used to mean
his or her

Speaking

4 Make full questions and answers based on 3.

A: *What should we do if the diver's location under water is unknown?*
B: *You should locate them and mark their position.*

Language

Must is used to show that an action is **necessary**, e.g. *Safety helmets must be worn at all times.*
Should is used to show that you're **recommending** or **suggesting** an action, e.g. *People think safety helmets should be orange. In my opinion, they should be yellow.*
Should + passive is used in the **recommendations** section of a report, e.g. *New first aid equipment should be purchased immediately.*

Reading

5 Read this email. Which section gives:

- *old information* (= what Jon already knows)?
- *new information* (= what Jon needs to know)?
- *action* (= what Jon needs to do)?

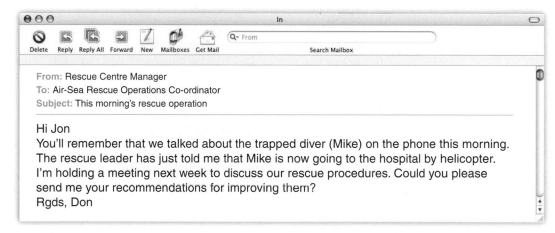

From: Rescue Centre Manager
To: Air-Sea Rescue Operations Co-ordinator
Subject: This morning's rescue operation

Hi Jon
You'll remember that we talked about the trapped diver (Mike) on the phone this morning. The rescue leader has just told me that Mike is now going to the hospital by helicopter. I'm holding a meeting next week to discuss our rescue procedures. Could you please send me your recommendations for improving them?
Rgds, Don

Writing

6 Write an email giving Jon's reply. Give old information, new information and action. Include six recommendations in the new information.

Choose six items from the table in 3, or give some of your own ideas for recommendations.

3 Directions

Start here   **1**   Identify these landmarks on the photo.

> flyover   gantry   motorway
> roundabout   slip road   underpass

Reading   **2**   Match the directions with the maps.

1   take the second turning on the left
2   take the third exit from the roundabout
3   turn right at the T-junction
4   come out of the building and turn right
5   go straight ahead at the crossroads
6   leave the motorway by the slip road and turn left at the roundabout
7   go over the bridge and take the first road on the right
8   come out of the car park and turn left under the flyover

Language

First describe the situation …	then give the instruction
There is a STOP sign at the end of the road.	Turn left here.
There are two sets of traffic lights on this road.	Turn right at the second set.
When you come out of the station,	turn right into Market Street.
You'll see a police station on your left.	Don't turn left here. Take the second turning on the left.
If you cross a bridge over the river, you've gone too far.	Do a U-turn. Go back across the bridge. Then take the first turning on the right.

Reading **3** Read this email and mark TurboTech on the map.

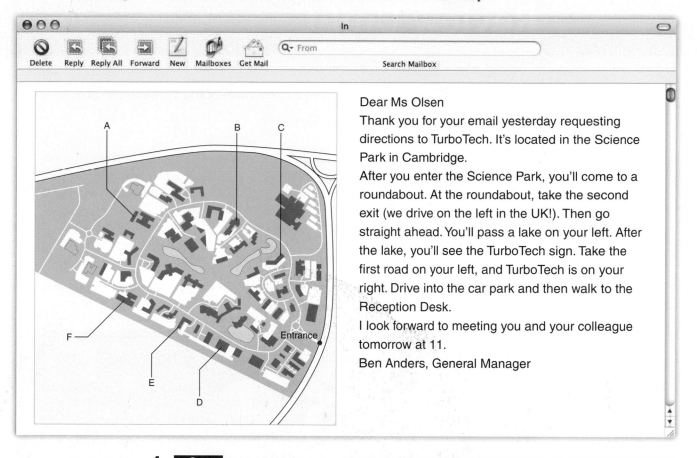

Dear Ms Olsen

Thank you for your email yesterday requesting directions to TurboTech. It's located in the Science Park in Cambridge.

After you enter the Science Park, you'll come to a roundabout. At the roundabout, take the second exit (we drive on the left in the UK!). Then go straight ahead. You'll pass a lake on your left. After the lake, you'll see the TurboTech sign. Take the first road on your left, and TurboTech is on your right. Drive into the car park and then walk to the Reception Desk.

I look forward to meeting you and your colleague tomorrow at 11.

Ben Anders, General Manager

Listening **4** ▶ 🎵 18 Listen to these telephone directions and mark the Engineering Department and the Sports Centre on the map.

Note: the university is in a country which drives on the left.

Speaking **5** Work in pairs, A and B. Give each other telephone directions to places on the map in 4.

Student A.
Turn to page 112.

Student B.
Turn to page 114.

Task **6** Work in pairs. List three local places you know.

- Tell your partner how to get there.
- Listen to your partner's directions and draw sketch maps.
- Exchange maps with your partner and check the details.

Review Unit C

1 Complete the sentences. Use the correct form of the verbs in the box.

> carry   convert   detect   start   treat

1 Jump leads are used for _____ a car with a flat battery.
2 The purpose of a hydrophone is to _____ signals under water.
3 The function of a transducer is to _____ energy from one form to another.
4 A first aid kit should only be used for _____ minor injuries.
5 A forklift truck must be used to _____ boxes around the warehouse.

2 Work in pairs. Discuss with your partner. What do you think is the function of each item of the diver's equipment?

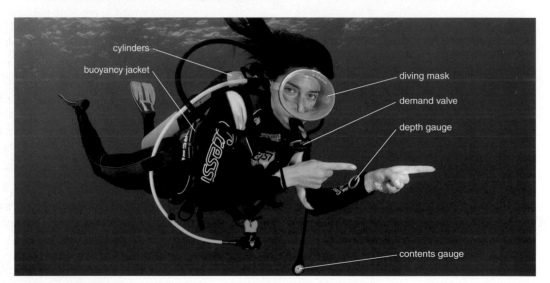

3 Take turns with your partner to describe the function of each item of equipment. Use the correct form of the verbs.

	Equipment	Function	
1	demand valve	control the flow of oxygen to the diver	(for)
2	cylinders	store oxygen under high pressure	(used to)
3	contents gauge	indicate the amount of oxygen in the cylinders	(present simple)
4	cylinders	transport oxygen with the diver	(used for)
5	depth gauge	indicate the depth of the water	(designed to)
6	buoyancy jacket	support the diver in the water	(for)
7	diving mask	allow diver to see clearly under water	(designed to)
8	contents gauge	a kind of alarm clock for the diver	(act as)
9	demand valve	supply oxygen to the diver when he or she needs it	(present simple)
10	buoyancy jacket	a very strong lifejacket	(act as)

Examples. 1 The demand valve is for controlling the flow of oxygen to the diver.

4 Supply the questions in this interview about the Man Overboard alarm system on page 41.

- *So tell us about your invention. What's* (1) _____?
- ○ It's called a 'digital-sonar alarm system' for boats.
- *And what's* (2) _____?
- ○ Well, it's for finding people when they fall off a boat into the water.
- *I see. And how* (3) _____?
- ○ Well, when the person falls into the water, a sensor on the pod sends a sonar signal to the hydrophone.
- *Hold on a minute. What exactly* (4) _____?
- ○ A hydrophone is a transducer which can detect signals under water.
- *I see. So who* (5) _____ for?
- ○ It's designed for everyone on the boat. The crew and their family.
- *OK, so tell me about the pod. What shape* (6) _____?
- ○ Well, it's shaped a bit like an egg.
- *And how* (7) _____?
- ○ It's quite small. It's about 15 cm long.
- *Where* (8) _____?
- ○ You wear it on your belt. It has a clip.
- *What* (9) _____?
- ○ It's made of a very tough polymer.
- *What* (10) _____?
- ○ It's a very bright colour, usually yellow or red.

5 What do you think these are for? Discuss with a partner.

6 Write a description of the four devices in 5. Describe (a) their appearance and (b) their function.

7 Make definitions.

1	an MP3 player	instrument	loosen and tighten nuts on wheels
2	fibreglass	system	repair underwater pipes and machines
3	artificial respiration	tool	powered by electricity from a solar panel
4	GPS	technician	download and play music from a computer
5	a sub-sea mechanic	vehicle	use satellites to locate your position
6	a solar-powered car	procedure	calculate diver's depth in the water
7	a wheel wrench	device	used for making hulls of boats
8	a depth gauge	material	help a casualty to breathe

Example. 1 An MP3 player is a device which downloads and plays music from a computer.

8 Write a reply to this email.
Note: the campus is in a country which drives on the right.

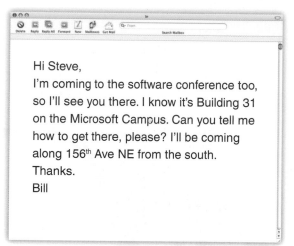

Hi Steve,
I'm coming to the software conference too, so I'll see you there. I know it's Building 31 on the Microsoft Campus. Can you tell me how to get there, please? I'll be coming along 156th Ave NE from the south.
Thanks.
Bill

9 Change these instructions into the passive.

1 You must carry two oxygen cylinders at all times during a dive.

_____

2 All staff have to wear lifejackets on board this oil rig.

_____

3 You must not stack boxes or crates in the aisles.

_____

4 You need to freeze all this food before you send it to the warehouse.

_____

5 Workers should never use forklift trucks as people carriers.

_____

6 You have to push trucks down a ramp. You must never pull them down.

_____

Example. 1 Two oxygen cylinders must be carried at all times during a dive.

10 Work in pairs, A and B.

Student A
1   Turn to page 112. Describe the object and ask Student B to draw it. Then check B's drawing. Does it look like your object?
2   Listen to Student B's description of an object, and draw it from their description. Show your drawing to B.

Student B
1   Listen to Student A's description of an object, and draw it from their description. Show your drawing to A.
2   Turn to page 115. Describe your object and ask Student A to draw it. Then check A's drawing. Does it look like your object?

11 Work in pairs. Discuss these questions about the fire extinguisher. Make notes of your answers.

- Should this device be used to put out electrical fires? Why/ Why not?
- What are (a) the cylinder and (b) the siphon made of?
- What properties do these materials have? Why are these properties important here?
- What function(s) does the valve have?
- What is the purpose of the rod? Why does it have a sharp point?
- How do you activate the extinguisher?
- What happens when you activate it? How does it work?
- What forces the water to rise up the siphon?
- How do you think you should hold and move the extinguisher when you are fighting a fire?
- What safety rules do you need when using a fire extinguisher?

12 With your partner, produce a safety poster about this type of extinguisher. Use your notes and add any other information you know.

Project **13** Find out about an important device or piece of equipment used in your technical field.

- Note down the key information.
- Prepare a short talk.
- Describe the device or equipment to the class.

1 Technical support

Start here

1 What problems have you had with computers? What were your solutions?

2 Work with a partner. Decide on the best solutions to these computer problems.

1 You can't log into your company network from home. Your password is rejected.
2 The image on your monitor is too large, and you can't see the whole page.
3 You can open your incoming emails, but you can't open their attachments.
4 A website says CLICK HERE TO SEE PHOTO. You click, but nothing happens.
5 You can't get a wireless connection between your computer and your router.
6 Now you have the wireless connection between your computer and your router, but you can't access the Internet. A message says LIMITED OR NO CONNECTIVITY.

Listening

3 🔊 **19** Lisa is an IT support technician in a large company. Her colleagues are trying to connect their home computers to the company network. They phone Lisa with their problems. Listen and complete Lisa's report.

CALL	PROBLEM	DIAGNOSIS	SOLUTION
1	Network rejects password	D3	S2
2	Can't see full page on screen; icons too large		
3	Can't open email attachments		
4	Click on link, but photo doesn't appear		
5	Can't connect computer wirelessly with router		
6	Can't access internet through wireless connection		

DIAGNOSIS CODE

D1	computer has different IP address from router
D2	electronic devices interfere with connection
D3	network system remembers wrong password
D4	wrong screen resolution settings
D5	firewall blocks pop-ups
D6	security level in email program is too high

SOLUTION CODE

S1	reboot the router and computer
S2	uncheck the REMEMBER PASSWORD box
S3	increase the screen resolution to correct setting
S4	switch off BLOCK POP-UP ADVERTS in firewall
S5	move the router to a different location
S6	lower the security level for attachments

4 ▶ **20** Listen to how Lisa diagnoses the problem. Complete the statements with the verbs in the box.

could	may	might	must

1 You _____ have checked the REMEMBER PASSWORD box.
2 Your computer _____ be using the wrong screen resolution settings.
3 Your email program _____ be blocking the attachments.
4 Your firewall _____ be blocking the pop-ups.
5 Another electronic device _____ be interfering with the connection.
6 You _____ have given the computer a different IP address from the router.

5 Which statements in 4 show that Lisa thinks her diagnosis is

- certainly correct? Write *C* after the statement.
- possibly correct? Write *P* after the statement.

6 ▶ **21** Listen to how Lisa suggests a solution. Complete the statements. Use the correct form of the verbs in the box.

could	don't	lower	suggest	try	type

1 Now try _____ in the correct password.
2 Try _____ your security level.
3 Well, you _____ move the phone away. Or why _____ you move the router around?
4 I _____ you _____ moving the router to a different location.

Language

Diagnosing a problem
- present possibility: *may/might/could* + *be*/present continuous, e.g. *The file may/might/could be too large.*
- present certainty: *must* + *be*/present continuous, e.g. *The firewall must be blocking the attachments.*
- past possibility: *must/may/might* + present perfect, e.g. *You may/might have broken it.*
- past certainty: *must* + present perfect, e.g. *You must have broken it.*

Suggesting a solution
- *try* + verb + *-ing*. *Try clicking on the 'undo' button.*
- *Why don't you ...? Why don't you click on the 'undo' button?*
- *could. You could click on the 'undo' button.*

---

7 Rephrase these. Use language from above.

1 *Diagnosis*: your switch is probably broken. *Suggestion*: change it
2 *D*: it's possible your cable is loose. *S*: push it firmly into the socket
3 *D*: you are definitely using the wrong IP address *S*: reboot the router
4 *D*: perhaps the program has frozen *S*: press CTRL-ALT-DEL
5 *D*: the mouse has definitely stopped working *S*: disconnect and reconnect
6 *D*: it's certain your file is too large for the disk *S*: compress it

Example: 1 Your switch might be broken. Try changing it.

2 Reporting to clients

Start here   **1**   How can architects make tall buildings safer in fires or other emergencies? Brainstorm some ideas in groups.

Task   **2**   Discuss these ideas for safer skyscrapers with your group.

- discuss the purpose of the ideas on the diagram
- draw up and complete a table like this

Ideas for making skyscrapers safer in fires and emergencies		
Idea	**Purpose**	
(a) CCTV cameras	to check everyone's location; to allow controllers to monitor the situation	
(b) parachutes	to allow people to escape quickly from the top floors	

(l) gaps between beams and columns

(k) skybridges

(j) fireproof lifts

(i) stronger sprinklers (with backup power and water)

(h) magnetic shaft*

(g) sensors (of smoke, heat, strain)

(f) wider doors

(m) wider stairs (reinforced with steel)

(n) loudspeakers

(a) CCTV cameras

(b) parachutes

(c) fireproof ceilings

(d) control centre (away from building)

(e) fire drills

* people put on magnetic lifejackets and jump into shaft

3   Discuss these questions with your group and add notes to your table in 2:

- Which safety features will work?
- Which ones will not work, or be too difficult to install?
- Discuss the reasons.

4   Present your group's decisions to the class.

Reading **5** Read this covering letter and answer the questions below.

1 Who is (a) the client (b) the contractor?
2 What did the client ask the contractor to do, and when did he ask it?
3 What has the contractor done?
4 Where is the contractor's report?
5 What does the contractor ask the client to do?
6 Which words introduce good news?

Commas are optional:
Dear Mr Hu,
Yours sincerely,

SAFETY DESIGNS LTD

Mr John Hu
Director
Hu Constructions Pte Ltd

Dear Mr Hu
<u>Safety upgrading of Hu Building</u>
Thank you for your letter of 24th January authorising us to do the above work.
I am pleased to inform you that the work was completed last month. Our report is attached.
Please let me know if you need clarification of any of the points in the report.
Yours sincerely

Pierre Van Ek

Director
enc. *Report on Safety Modifications to Hu Building.*

6 Read the contractor's report. Write a number from the diagram in 2 next to each job report.

Summary report from Safety Designs Ltd
The following jobs were carried out in the Hu Building during January – October:

1 Three walkways were built between the towers to allow people to cross over. (_____)
2 The width of stairs was increased by 25 cm to allow more people to use them. (_____)
3 Fire-resistant material was placed between floors to stop fires from spreading. (_____)
4 Exits on the ground floor were widened by 1 m to allow people to escape more easily. (_____)
5 Elevators were covered with fire-resistant material to protect them. (_____)
6 Structural beams were shortened by 8 cm to allow them to expand in a fire. (_____)
7 Smoke detectors were installed to give early warning of fire. (_____)
8 No equipment for jumping was provided since we decided it was impractical. (_____)

7 Underline examples of the passive in the summary report in 6.

Example: 1 Three walkways <u>were built</u> between the towers …

Language

| The building work | was | completed | last month. |
| Three walkways | were | built | between the towers. |

8 Change the sentences in the report in 6 into the active.

Example: 1 We built three walkways between the towers to allow people to cross over.

Speaking **9** Refer to the table your group completed in 2. In your group, roleplay a meeting between client and contractor.

Appoint one member of your group to be the client, John Hu. The other group members are a team of contractors working for Safety Designs Ltd. The contractors have now carried out the work they specified in the table in 2.

In the meeting, the client asks the contractors what changes they made to the building, why they made/did not make the changes and other questions about dimensions, materials, etc. The contractors answer the client's questions.

3 Dealing with complaints

Start here

1 What are the most common customer complaints in your technical field?

2 How should staff deal with a complaint from a customer? Make some guidelines for staff (in note form).

Listening

3 ▶ 🎧 22 Listen to this phone call from a customer with a complaint. Note down the details in the complaints form.

Date and time of call	10.45 16/03
Name of customer	
Order number	
Description of goods	
Model number	
Details of complaint	
Solution offered	☐ *replace* ☐ *repair* ☐ *refund* ☐ *reduce*
Customer response	☐ *accept* ☐ *reject*

4 Listen again to the phone call. Look at the company handbook below. Which procedures are (a) ***followed*** (b) ***broken*** by the staff?

Procedure for dealing with a telephone complaint from a customer

1 be friendly, polite and helpful
2 listen carefully
3 show sympathy with the customer's problem, but don't admit the company's fault
4 summarise what the customer has told you, and check that you have understood correctly
5 record the details and collect the evidence (e.g. receipts or damaged goods)
6 offer a solution (*repair* the item, *replace* it, *refund* the money or *reduce* the price of the next purchase)

Task

5 Work in pairs, A and B. Roleplay a phone call between service staff and a customer with a complaint. Before you start, study the audio script of the phone call in 3 on page 124.

Student A. You're the customer. Make notes about your device and what is wrong with it. Include a model name, number and an order number. Then call customer services.

Student B. You work in customer service. Draw up a customer complaints form like the one in 3. Then take the call from the customer and deal with their complaint.

6 Describe the damage to the suitcase.

| broken | burnt | cracked | crushed | dented | split | torn | twisted |

corner
edge
surface

label

Reading   **7**   Read this reply to a customer's letter of complaint and answer the questions.

Dear Ms Beck

Thank you for your letter complaining about your DVD player from our store. I was sorry to hear that the top surface of the machine was scratched and the edge was cracked.

Unfortunately, we do not have any more DVD players in stock at the moment. However, I am pleased to inform you that we will give you your money back in full. In addition, as a gesture of goodwill, we will give you a 10% discount off your next purchase from our store.

I would like to apologise for the inconvenience you have experienced. Please do not hesitate to contact me if you have any further queries.

Yours sincerely

Robert Wilson

Store Manager

1   What did the customer complain about?
2   What does the writer offer to do?
3   Which words (a) show sympathy (b) give an apology?
4   Which words introduce (a) good news (b) bad news?

Writing   **8**   You are the Manager of IT Online Ltd. Reply to this letter.

The Manager, IT Online Ltd

Dear Sir or Madam
I wish to complain about the Mace notebook computer which I ordered from your online store last month (order number 60335/01). The computer was delivered only yesterday. When I opened the box, the adapter was missing. This is very poor service indeed. I look forward to hearing from you.

Peter Bradwell

1 Wave power

Start here

1 Brainstorm in small groups. Make notes or draw simple diagrams.

How can the energy of sea waves be converted into electrical power?

Task

2 Study this diagram. It shows one method of converting wave energy into electrical power. With your group

- decide how it works
- explain your group's ideas to the rest of the class

Vocabulary

3 Complete this text with the correct motion words.

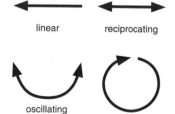

linear   reciprocating

oscillating   rotary

There are four basic motions. First, there is (1) _____ motion. This is movement in a straight line, and in one direction. Secondly, there is (2) _____ motion, which is two-way movement backwards and forwards or up and down (like a piston) in a straight line. The third type is (3) _____ motion, which swings from side to side (like a pendulum). Finally, there is (4) _____ motion, which is motion in a circular direction, like the shaft of a wind turbine.

4 Match the numbered arrows in the diagram in 2 with the motion words in 3.

5 Complete these sentences. Use the present simple of the verbs in the box.

clockwise   anti-clockwise

1 Propeller shafts _____.
2 A car engine piston _____.
3 Pendulums _____.
4 When you tighten a screw, it _____ clockwise.

| oscillate   reciprocate |
| rotate |

Scanning **6** Practise your speed reading. Look for the information you need on the SPEED SEARCH pages (118–119). Try to be the first to complete the task.

Task: Find out five advantages (or benefits) of the wave energy converter.

Listening **7** ▶ 🔊 **23** Listen to this presentation about the Wave Energy Converter, and complete the listener's notes.

WAVE ENERGY CONVERTER

DEFINITION: system for converting (1)_____ from sea waves into electrical power
LOCATION: fixed to the (2)_____
MAIN COMPONENTS: a flexible disc, a lever, a (3)_____ which takes in sea water, a set of (4)_____, many sea water pipes, a (5)_____ on the land
MAIN SPECIFICATIONS: 4.6 m (H) x (6)_____ m (L); pipe (7)_____ mm (W); pressure (8)_____ kPa (1000 psi); can generate (9)_____ kW of electricity
OPERATION: wave oscillates → pushes disc (10)_____ → lever oscillates → reciprocating pumps push water through pipe at (11)_____ pressure → turbine (12)_____ → generates electricity
BENEFITS: Wave energy is a (13)_____ energy resource; uses no fossil fuels

---

Task **8** Work in small groups. Find out about one of these wave energy systems. Prepare a presentation about your system.

Wave Energy Buoy

Wave Power Station

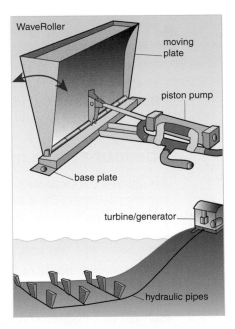

WaveRoller

Group 1. Turn to page 112 for your notes about the *Wave Energy Buoy*. (1)
Group 2. Turn to page 114 for your notes about the *Wave Power Station*. (2)
Group 3. Turn to page 116 for your notes about the *WaveRoller*. (3)

9 With your group, give a presentation about your system to the class. Answer questions from the class.

Writing **10** Write a description of your group's system, explaining how it works.

2 Engines

Start here **1** Work with a partner or in small groups. Draw arrows to show all the movements in this diagram of an internal-combustion engine cylinder.

2 Describe the motion of all the moving parts in the diagram. Use the words in the box.

> linear   oscillating   reciprocating   rotary

3 Explain what causes the movements of

- the valves
- the piston
- the crankshaft

Internal-combustion engine cylinder

Task **4** With your partner or group, number these diagrams in the correct order.

Before the cycle begins

Fuel is ignited

Reading **5** Read this description of the four-stroke cycle. Check your answers to 4.

The four-stroke internal combustion cycle

BEFORE THE CYCLE BEGINS. The cycle begins at *top dead centre* (TDC). Here the piston is furthest away from the crankshaft. There are four *strokes* of the piston.

INTAKE STROKE. The crankshaft rotates. This makes the piston move down the cylinder, away from the valves. At the same time, the cam above the intake valve rotates. This makes the valve move downwards,
5 which opens the intake port. As the piston moves down, fuel is sucked into the cylinder through this inlet.

COMPRESSION STROKE. As the crankshaft rotates, it makes the piston move up the chamber towards the valves. Simultaneously, the cam above the intake valve rotates and allows it to close. Both valves are now closed. As the piston moves up towards the valves, it compresses the fuel.

IGNITION. Now the piston is once again at TDC. The compressed fuel is ignited by the spark plug, and there
10 is a small explosion at the top of the cylinder.

POWER STROKE. Immediately after this, the gases expand in the cylinder, which pushes the piston downwards. This makes the crankshaft rotate and provides torsion to drive the wheels of the vehicle.

EXHAUST STROKE. As the crankshaft rotates, it pushes the piston up the cylinder. At the same time, the cam above the exhaust valve pushes the valve downwards. This opens the exhaust port, and the burnt gases are
15 pushed out.

The cycle is repeated thousands of times per minute.

6 What do these words refer to?

    1 *which* (line 5)   a) the valve b) the rotation of the cam
                               c) the movement of the valve
    2 *it* (line 7)   a) the cam b) the intake valve c) the rotation of the cam
    3 *this* (line 11)   a) the small explosion b) the top of the cylinder
    4 *which* (line 11) a) the cylinder b) the expansion of the gases
    5 *This* (line 14)   a) the cam b) the valve c) the movement of the valve

7 Find words in the text that mean the same as these phrases.

    1 at the same time (one word)
    2 twisting force (one word)
    3 inlet which allows fuel to enter the cylinder (two words)
    4 device which moves to allow gases to escape (two words)

Language

When often indicates that two actions happen in sequence, i.e. immediately after the other, e.g. *When the spark plug ignites, the gases explode.*

As often indicates that two actions happen simultaneously, i.e. both at the same time, e.g. *As the piston moves up, it compresses the fuel.*

When or *as* can sometimes be used with the same meaning when it's difficult to decide if two actions are simultaneous or in rapid sequence, e.g. *When/As the brake pedal is pressed, the piston pushes the oil along the brake pipe.*

---

8 Join each group of sentences into a single sentence. Use ***when/as*** and ***which***. Do not use the words in italics.

    1 The piston moves up. *At the same time*, the exhaust valve opens. This lets the burnt gases escape.
    2 The spark plug ignites the fuel. *Immediately afterwards*, there is an explosion. This makes the piston move down with great force.
    3 The camshaft rotates. *Simultaneously*, the cam pushes the intake valve downwards. This allows the fuel to enter the cylinder.
    4 The piston moves away from the valves. *Immediately after this*, it creates a vacuum in the cylinder. This sucks the fuel in.
    5 The piston moves up towards the valves. *Soon afterwards,* it puts the fuel under high pressure. This helps the gases to expand rapidly after ignition.
    6 The cam pushes the exhaust valve down. *At the same time*, the piston moves up towards it. This forces the burnt gases out of the engine.

    Example: 1 As the piston moves up, the exhaust valve opens, which lets the burnt gases escape.

Writing **9** This is a diagram of an internal combustion engine that uses hydrogen as a fuel. Describe this engine and explain how it works. Explain the benefits of this kind of engine.

3 Cooling and heating

Start here

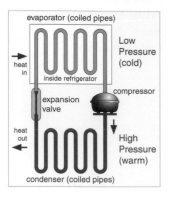

evaporator (coiled pipes)

Low Pressure (cold)

heat in

inside refrigerator

expansion valve

compressor

heat out

High Pressure (warm)

condenser (coiled pipes)

1 Discuss this question in groups. Which two scientific principles are refrigerators based on?

1 For every action there is an equal but opposite reaction.
2 When you compress a gas, it condenses. When you decompress a liquid, it evaporates.
3 The upthrust is equal to the weight of the displaced fluid.
4 As a gas condenses, it gives out heat. As a liquid evaporates, it absorbs (takes in) heat.

2 With your group, make notes about what happens to the fluid during a refrigeration cycle. Use the two principles from 1.

GAS	condense > < evaporate	LIQUID	solidify > < melt	SOLID

Reading **3** Read this description of a heat pump, and complete the diagram below.

- draw an arrow on the pipes to show the direction of flow of the fluid
- delete the words *high* or *low* in the brackets

HEAT PUMPS

A heat pump is an electrical device that pumps heat from one place to another. During cold weather, it extracts heat from the outside air, and transfers it into the building. During hot weather, the heat pump reverses this operation, and transfers heat from inside the building to the outside.

The machine is based on the two principles of the refrigeration cycle: (1) when a gas is compressed, it condenses, and gives out heat, and (2) when a liquid is expanded, it evaporates, and absorbs (or takes in) heat.

The main parts of a heat pump are a compressor, an expansion valve, two fans, a reversing valve and two sets of coils, one on the outside and the other on the inside of the building. The coils are thin pipes which are bent in a U shape many times. They can absorb and give out heat.

The compressor pumps a special fluid called a refrigerant around the coils. The refrigerant is under high pressure as it flows from the compressor to the condenser. As the fluid passes around the condenser coils, it gives out heat to the surrounding air. The fluid then passes through the expansion valve. Here the pressure is suddenly reduced and the fluid expands. This makes it evaporate. As the fluid passes around the evaporator coils, it absorbs heat from the surrounding air, making it cold. Then the fluid flows back to the compressor.

HEATING OPERATION

In cold weather, the outside coil acts as the evaporator and the inside coil acts as the condenser. The fluid in the evaporator is under low pressure, and so it evaporates. The fan pulls the outside air over the evaporator and the fluid absorbs heat from it. The compressor then pumps the heated fluid into the building under high pressure to the condenser. The second fan blows air over the condenser, and the heated air is blown into the building.

The heat pump: heating operation

fluid under (*high/low*) pressure

fluid under (*high/low*) pressure

outside coil

reversing valve

inside coil

fan

compressor

fan

expansion valve

fluid under (*high/low*) pressure

fluid under (*high/low*) pressure

4 Match the parts with their definitions.

1	expansion valve	a)	coiled pipes that give out heat to the surrounding air
2	coils	b)	a pump which compresses the refrigerant
3	condenser	c)	a device that decompresses the refrigerant
4	refrigerant	d)	a fluid which evaporates at a low temperature
5	evaporator	e)	pipes that carry the refrigerant around the system
6	compressor	f)	coiled pipes that extract heat from the surrounding air

Vocabulary

5 Make a table for all the words in the box. Use a dictionary if necessary.

> compress   condense   decompress   evaporate   extract   operate   refrigerate

Verb	Concept noun	Agent noun
compress	compression	compressor

Writing

6 Continue and complete this description of the cooling operation of the heat pump.

Cooling operation
During hot weather, the operation of the heat pump is reversed. The reversing valve changes the machine from a heater to an air conditioner. The outside coil then acts as …

The heat pump: cooling operation

Task

7 Work in small groups. Discuss this geothermal pump. Make notes about

- its function
- how it works
- how it is different from the heat pump

The ground collector is buried in the ground outside the building

8 Write a description of the geothermal pump and how it works.

1 Complete these phone conversations. Use the correct form of the verbs in brackets.

1 (remember / check / uncheck / type)

A: *I can't log into my company network. My password was rejected.*

B: Your network system must be (1) *remembering* the wrong password. You might have (2) *checked* the **REMEMBER PASSWORD** box. Try (3) _____ this feature. Then try (4) _____ in the correct password again.

2 (block / lower / open)

A: *I can't open my email attachments.*

B: Your email program must be (5) _____ the attachments. Try (6) _____ your security settings. Then you can try (7) _____ the attachments again.

3 (block / switch off / empty)

A: *I click on a link on a web page, but the link doesn't pop up.*

B: Your firewall might have (8) _____ the pop-up. Try (9) _____ the **BLOCK POP-UPS** option in your firewall and then try (10) _____ your cache.

4 (interfere / take / move)

A: *I can't get a wireless connection between my computer and my router.*

B: A cordless phone or other device might be (11) _____ with the connection. Try (12) _____ the phone away. Or why don't you (13) _____ the router to another location?

5 (use / reboot / reboot / reboot)

A: *I can't access the internet with my wireless router.*

B: The router must be (14) _____ the wrong IP address. Why don't you (15) _____ the router first. If that doesn't work, try (16) _____ the computer and then you could (17) _____ the router again.

2 A hotline technician made these notes of phone conversations with customers. Roleplay the phone conversations with a partner.

1

PROBLEM: computer not starting

CHECK FIRST: plugged into wall? plugged into power strip? power strip on?

PERHAPS: circuit in power strip broken

TRY THIS: plug into different outlet

2

PROBLEM: printer not working

CHECK FIRST: printer plugged in? turned on? paper jam? no paper in printer? on a network? logged into network correctly?

PERHAPS: printer not recognising computer

TRY THIS: log on again

OR THIS: check printer icon on taskbar

3

PROBLEM: monitor screen blank

CHECK FIRST: monitor turned on? green light near power button? monitor connected properly to computer?

PERHAPS: connector cable loose

TRY THIS: tighten all cables

PROBLEM: still blank

PERHAPS: brightness/contrast buttons turned down

TRY THIS: adjust buttons on monitor

3 What do you think could have caused the events in the photos to happen? Tell the class.

4 Discuss how a two-stroke engine works with a partner.

5 Put these sentences into the correct order.

Two-stroke engine: the upstroke

As a result, fresh fuel is sucked into the crankcase.
The vacuum opens the fuel valve.
When it reaches the top, the spark plug fires.
This compresses the fuel in the cylinder.
As the crankshaft rotates, it drives the piston up. **1**
Then the downstroke begins.
At the same time, it creates a vacuum in the crankcase.
Meanwhile, the piston moves up towards the top of the cylinder.

6 Use the information in these notes to write a paragraph describing the **downstroke** of the two-stroke engine.

Use *when* or *as* where possible to join two lines together. You can also use other words such as *meanwhile*.

Two-stroke engine: the downstroke	
1 spark plug fires	7 piston uncovers exhaust port
2 fuel ignites	8 piston reaches bottom of cylinder
3 this drives piston down	9 piston uncovers transfer port
4 piston moves down	10 fuel flows from crankcase
5 compresses fuel in crankcase	11 fuel flows into cylinder
6 piston moves down more	12 fresh fuel pushes out exhaust gas

Begin: When the spark plug fires, the fuel ignites. This drives the piston down. As it moves …

7 Complete the sentences with the correct form of the verbs in brackets.

1 My new washing machine has _____. (break down)
2 My new car was _____ yesterday. The mirrors are _____.
(deliver / crack)
3 You have _____ me the wrong shipment. (send)
4 I _____ two CDs from you this morning by post. They're both
_____. (receive / scratch)
5 We _____ two generators last month, but you have not
_____ them. (order / deliver)
6 I _____ the motorbike a month ago, but the brakes have already
_____ down. (buy / wear)

8 A safety inspector investigates a fire in a building, and writes a report from his notes. Complete the report. Use the passive throughout.

INSPECTOR'S NOTES

THINGS TO DO: examine the site of the fire
… inspect joints and connections … test
the main lift … measure gaps between beams
… take away and test parts of the wall …
inspect all fire exits

DAMAGE: the fire destroys four storeys …
it shears three metal beams … it twists the
main column … it jams two lifts … it blocks
two fire exits … the heat cracks a large
water tank (for sprinklers)

I RECOMMEND: reinforce structural columns
… strengthen water tanks … provide backup
power system … install CCTV and monitors
… widen stairs … cover ceilings with fireproof
material

INSPECTOR'S REPORT

ACTIONS TAKEN
1 The site of the fire was examined.
2 Joints and connections were
inspected.
3 …

FINDINGS
1 Four storeys were destroyed by the
fire.
2 Three metal beams were sheared.
3 …

RECOMMENDATIONS
1 Structural columns should be
reinforced.
2 Water tanks should be strengthened.
3 …

9 You are the manager of Technik Ltd. Reply to this letter.

The Manager, Technik Ltd

Dear Sir or Madam

Hotspot washing machine: receipt no. TT/893/08

I am writing to complain about the Hotspot washing machine that I ordered from your
city centre shop two weeks ago. The washing machine was delivered ten days ago, and
it was installed by your service staff on the same day. It worked when the service man
switched it on, but when I switched it on again the next day, there was a loud crash,
and then the machine stopped. I called the service hotline, but there was no reply for
two days. Finally, I sent an email to customer services. The washing machine was taken
away this morning, one week late. I am not satisfied with the washing machine or the
service from your company. I look forward to hearing from you.

Misha Williams

10 Work in pairs or in small groups. Discuss the two types of Stirling engine. Decide how they work.

11 Write a description of the two engines, and how they work.

Project 12 Find out about an important engine or piece of equipment used in your industry. Get information about

- the principle behind it
- the function of the main parts
- how it works

13 Give a short talk about this to the class.

1 Sports data

Start here   **1**   What do you know about the Tour de France cycle race? Discuss in pairs.

- How long is the route (approximately)? How many days does it take?
- What do you think cyclists need to measure when they train for a race?

Reading   **2**   Read this blog and check your answers to 1.

BLOGS   DIRECTORY   CONTACT

Team4Tour

Posted: 27 November   Comment **here**

Hello. Welcome to Team4Tour, the blog of my cycling group. We're a team of six racing cyclists, and right now we're cycling around the Tour de France route, which is 3553 km. We're not competing in the actual race this year (maybe next year …). Right now, we're only practising the route. Click **here** to see a summary of the distances we hope to cover every day. We've brought some fantastic measurement devices with us (click **here** to see one). To see my bike maintenance schedule, click **here**.

Day 3. Now we've completed the third day, which means almost one sixth of the whole tour of twenty days! We're in Northern France, and we're going to have a rest day tomorrow …

DAY	DISTANCE	PERCENTAGE/FRACTION	DAY	DISTANCE	PERCENTAGE/FRACTION
3	604 km	17% almost one sixth	13	2309 km	65%
5	1030 km	29%	15	2700 km	76%
7	1386 km	39%	17	3162 km	89%
10	1954 km	55%	19	3410 km	96%

My measuring device has a 5-cm display which shows many different measurements. The most useful features are the *odometer* (to measure the distance I travel), the *tachometer* (for measuring my speed), the *altimeter* (which measures my altitude) and the *barometer* (for measuring atmospheric pressure). The speed and distance data are sent wirelessly from a sensor mounted on the front of the bike.

After every ride.* * *ride = day of cycling*	Inflate tyres. Make sure that they are at the correct pressure. Examine tyres for wear. Worn tyres cause accidents. Check that the quick-release levers on the wheel are tight. I don't want wheels to fall off!
After every third ride (or every 500 km, whichever is sooner)	Test brakes and gears. Check that they are adjusted correctly. Inspect the saddle. Ensure that it is tight and at the correct height. I don't want it to slip down.
Every tenth ride (or when bike is wet)	Wash and dry bike. Apply oil carefully to chain and gears. Check that there's no lubricant on the wheel rims, to prevent brakes from slipping.

3 Answer these questions on the text.

1 What instruments provide data to measure: (1) How fast am I cycling? (2) How far have I cycled today? (3) How high am I above sea level?
2 When you inspect the (1) tyres (2) quick-release levers (3) saddle (4) wheel rims, what problems are you trying to prevent?
3 A cyclist has completed 520 km in two days of cycling. Should he/she test the gears now?

Vocabulary **4** Match the sports measuring instruments with the other items in the table.

Measuring instrument	What is measured	Unit of measurement	Abbreviation
1 barometer	distance (cycling)	metres	km/h
2 tachometer	speed	seconds	m
3 odometer	height (above sea level)	beats per second	km
4 altimeter	rate of heart beat	kilopascals	bps
5 stop watch	weight	watts	s
6 heart rate monitor	power output	kilograms	W
7 power monitor	pressure	kilometres per hour	kPa
8 scales	time	kilometres	kg

5 Ask and answer questions about the table.

What do you use for measuring your power output? What does kPa stand for? What's the abbreviation for beats per second? What's a tachometer used for? What does a barometer measure?

6 What units of measurement and measuring instruments do you use in your technical field? Make a table. Use the headings from 4. Ask and answer questions about it, as in 5.

7 Complete the distance table in the blog in 2 with the words in the box. Use approximate fractions.

almost   approximately   just under   just over   more than   nearly

8 Make some statements using fractions about yourself, or about a topic which interests you.

Example: I've completed just under two thirds of my training.

Reading **9** Read the text and answer the questions below.

Notice singulars, plurals and hyphens (-)
at 3000-km intervals = at 3000-kilometre intervals
every 3000 km = every 3000 kilometres

Change the oil and filter and lubricate moving parts every six months, or at 6000-mile intervals, whichever is the sooner. Service the battery after 54 months or 54,000 miles, whichever is the sooner. The brakes should be inspected and serviced (if necessary) at three-month intervals or every 3000 miles, whichever is the sooner.

1 A car has done 54,000 miles but only 50 months. Should the battery be serviced now?
2 A car has done 30 months, and 28,256 miles. The driver has inspected the brakes nine times. The last time was three months ago. Should the brakes be inspected again now?

2 Sensors

Start here

1 Which of the following is *not* a sensor? Why not?

2 What other sensors can you think of?

3 With a partner, write a definition of a sensor. Use these or other words.

sensor, device, detect, change (n), environment, convert, data

Begin: A sensor is …

Reading

4 Discuss with your partner.

- What's happening here?
- What are the engineers trying to measure?
- What kind of sensors are used?

5 Read this article and complete the statements below using these words: *acceleration*, *load*, *motion*.

Two different crash test dummies are used in standard European vehicle crash tests. The first dummy is used for front impact crashes, and the second one is a side impact crash dummy. The dummies, which are made of steel, aluminium and rubber, contain many sensors.

Three types of sensing equipment are used: *acceleration sensors*, *load sensors* and *motion sensors*. The dummy heads contain three accelerometers (single direction acceleration sensors) which are set at right angles (forward–backward, up–down, and left–right). The dummy necks contain load sensors to detect the bending forces, shear forces and tension forces, which put pressure on the neck in a crash. The dummy legs contain load sensors, which measure the bending, shear, compression and tension forces on the leg.

In addition, a front impact crash test dummy has steel ribs fitted with motion sensors which record front rib movement. A side impact dummy has motion sensors which record side chest deflection (or inward movement), and load sensors to measure compression forces on the chest.

Three types of sensors are used in crash test dummies:

1 _____ sensors measure deflection (inward movement) of a body part during a crash.

2 _____ sensors measure how much a body part increases or decreases speed during a crash.

3 _____ sensors measure the force or pressure on different body parts during a crash.

Vocabulary   **6**   Match the diagrams with (a) the names of the forces and (b) their descriptions.

(a) bending, compression, shear, tension, torsion

(b) squeezing or pressing together; sliding in opposite directions; stretching or pulling apart; twisting; squeezing one side + stretching the other side

Language   Noun + noun combinations are very common in technical English.

Examples: acceleration sensors (= sensors which measure acceleration); *vehicle crash tests* (= tests which crash a vehicle to measure its safety); *a side impact crash dummy* (= a dummy which measures the impact from the side in a crash).

7   Find phrases in the article in 5 which mean the same as these. All the words in the phrases must be nouns.

1   forces which pull something apart
2   sensors which detect movement or motion
3   deflection of the side of the chest
4   crashes which are caused by an impact from the front
5   a dummy which is used for testing the impact of a crash from the front

8   Expand these phrases. You can change words and add information.

1   a gas flow meter = *a meter which measures/for measuring the flow of gas (along a pipe)*
2   an engine speed dial = _____
3   a tyre pressure gauge = _____
4   a bass volume indicator = _____
     _____
5   an air pressure sensor = _____
     _____
6   a fuel intake port = _____

9   Make full sentence definitions from 8.

Example: 1 A gas flow meter is a meter which measures the flow of gas along a pipe.

gas flow meter

engine speed dial

tyre pressure gauge

bass volume indicator

Task   **10**   List some sensors used in your industry. Complete a table like this one. If possible, work in small groups with others from the same industry.

Industry: civil engineering and construction		
Name of sensor	**Function/Use**	**Application**
strain gauge	to measure deformation of structures	high-rise buildings, bridges, roads

11   Explain to the class about the sensors you have listed in your table.

In the field of civil engineering and construction, strain gauges are used for measuring the deformation of structures. They're used in high-rise buildings, bridges and roads, for example.

3 Positioning

Start here

1 Work in pairs. What do these systems calculate? Choose the most important one for each system.

distance, speed, location, height, depth

Reading

2 The footnotes on this web page are in the wrong order. Write the footnote numbers in the spaces.

What is GPS?

GPS stands for the Global Positioning System. It can tell you **your precise location**[1] anywhere on (or above) the Earth to within six metres.

5   A group of 24 or more satellites orbit the Earth at an altitude of 11,000 miles. Every 12 hours, a satellite makes an orbit, or one complete cycle in space around the Earth. The satellites transmit signals to receivers on the ground.

10   The user has a GPS receiver, which detects the signals from the satellites, and calculates **their distance**[2] from the receiver. Receivers can be held in your hand or mounted in a vehicle, such as a car or ship. A hand-held receiver is about the

15 size of a mobile phone, but the newer models are even smaller. For instance, you can now buy one which is as small as an MP3 player.

How does the system work?

The satellites know **their precise position**[3] in

20 their own orbits. Each satellite sends a signal to the receiver at the speed of light. This signal tells the receiver its exact location. In addition, it tells the receiver **the transmission time**[4] of the signal.

How does the receiver calculate how far it is

25 **from the satellite?**

It subtracts the time when the signal was received (T_1) from the time when it was sent (T_2). Then it multiplies this number by the speed of light (c). This gives the distance (D) from the receiver to the

30 satellite. However, to find out your exact location (that is, your longitude, latitude, and altitude), your receiver needs signals from at least three satellites.

Why do you need at least three satellites to tell you where you are?

35 Each satellite transmits a different position and time signal to the receiver. The receiver is able to calculate its exact location (to within 6 m) by comparing the three different signals.

FOOTNOTES

(_____) in other words, *when it was sent*

(_____) that is, *how far away they are*

(_____) or, *exactly where you are*

(_____) i.e., *exactly where they (the satellites) are*

3 Choose the correct calculation according to the text.

a) $D = (T_2 - T_1)/c$

c) $D = (T_2 - T_1) * c$

b) $T_1 - (T_2 * c) = D$

d) $T_2 - (T_1 * c) = D$

4 Choose the closest meaning for each word/phrase in the text. Choose from these meanings: *and*, *but*, *for example*, *in other words*.

1 *or* (line 7)

2 *such as* (line 13)

3 *For instance* (line 16)

4 *In addition* (line 22)

5 *However* (line 30)

6 *that is* (line 31)

to within 6 m = with a tolerance of ± 6 m

	Noun phrase
Please tell me I need to know This instrument can show you The computer calculates	your location. the depth of the river. the altitude of the planes.
	Indirect question
	where you are. how deep the river is. how high the planes are.

5 Replace the phrases in italics. Use the nouns in the box and add any necessary words.

altitude   depth   distance   height   length   location   speed   temperature   width

1 Please find out *where the ship is*, and *how fast she is going*.
2 Before you touch the liquid, you should check *how hot it is*.
3 I want to find out *how far away the plane is*, and *how high it is above sea level*.
4 Could you please tell me *how deep the river is* below the bridge.
5 I also need to know *how wide*, *how long* and *how high the bridge is*.

Example: 1 Please find out the location of the ship, and her speed.

6 Replace the phrases in italics. Use the word(s) in brackets.

1 All aeroplanes carry altimeters. These devices measure air pressure. From this reading, the altimeter can calculate *the height of the plane above sea level*. (how / high)
2 A submarine's pinger sends out a ping, or burst of sound, which is reflected back from ships in the sea. This allows the crew to find out *the location of the ships*. (where)
3 A lidar system can work out *the distance of a vehicle* from the device. It takes many readings as the vehicle approaches. From this it can calculate *the speed of the vehicle*. (how / far / fast)
4 An airport radar system sends out a sound signal which is reflected from an approaching plane. Since the system knows *the speed of the sound signal*, it can calculate *the distance of the plane* from the airport tower. (how / fast / far)

Example: 1 ... the altimeter can calculate how high the plane is above sea level.

Task **7** Work in groups.

- Brainstorm an everyday applications which use GPS. Choose one that interests you.
- Prepare a short presentation, showing how GPS works in the application.
- Present your group's ideas to the rest of the class.

Some examples of the use of GPS include: *police, fire and emergency medical services; forest fire prevention; surveying and construction; tunnel digging; bridge building; mining; company cars; delivery vans; dealing with environmental disasters such as oil spills in the sea; air-sea rescue services; agriculture; animal herding; tracking endangered species; hiking and camping; sailing.*

1 Properties

Start here 1 This is a bridge in a severe storm, minutes before it collapsed. Identify the forces acting on it. Use the words in the box.

> compression   shearing   tension   torsion

Scanning 2 Practise your speed reading. Look for the information you need on the SPEED SEARCH pages (118–119). Try to be the first to complete the task.

Task: Find information about the bridge in the photo in 1.
- What was the name of the bridge?
- In which year did it collapse?
- How strong was the wind?

Reading 3 Read these descriptions of tests and write the figure number in the gaps.

Fig. 1

Fig. 2

Fig. 3

Materials-testing: destructive tests

The purpose of the tensile strength test (**Fig. _____**) is to discover whether a material will *deform* (change shape) or break when it is pulled apart. The material is secured with two clamps, one at each end. The clamps are pulled apart with a specified force. The *yield point* (the point where the material deforms) and/or the *breaking point* (the point where the material breaks) is measured. This measurement shows you the tensile strength of the material.

The aim of the impact-resistance test (**Fig. _____**) is to find out whether a material will bend or break when it is struck with force. The bottom of the material is placed in a clamp, so that it stands vertically. A hammer strikes the material with a specified force. The yield point and/or the breaking point is measured. This indicates the impact resistance of the material.

The objective of the compressive strength test (**Fig. _____**) is to find out if a material will deform or break when it is compressed. The material is secured in a clamp between a fixed head and a moving head. The moving head presses down on the material and the load is increased. The yield point and/or the breaking point are measured. This indicates the compressive strength of the material.

4 Divide each paragraph in 3 into three sections. Use these headings.

- Objective   • Procedure   • Result

Example. **Objective.** *The purpose of the tensile strength test …* **Procedure.** *The material is secured …* **Result.** *This measurement shows you …*

Aim	*of*	Process	*is*	*to*	Verb	*if*	Phrase
The aim The purpose The objective	of	the test the investigation	is	to	find out discover	if whether	the metal bends. the plastic breaks.

5 Change these questions into statements about objectives. Use each word/phrase at least once.

> aim   discover   find out   investigation   objective   purpose   test

1 Does this metal deform easily when it is hammered?
2 Is this material elastic or plastic when it is stretched?
3 Does this metal break when you strike it with a force of 10,000 newtons?
4 Will this plastic withstand deformation when it is heated to 120°C?
5 Do these three types of ceramic melt when they are heated to over 500°C?
6 Will this concrete beam crack when it is compressed under a weight of 5 tonnes?

Example: 1 The purpose of the test is to discover if this metal deforms easily when it is hammered.

withstand = resist

Vocabulary

6 Underline the stressed syllable.

1 tens ile   tens ion
2 com press ive   com press ion
3 ri gid   ri gid i ty
4 flex i bil i ty   flex i ble
5 e las ti ci ty   e las tic
6 plas tic   plas ti ci ty

7 ▶ 🔘 24 Listen and check your answers.

8 Make a table like this. Use all the words from 6.

Noun	Adjective	Noun	Adjective
tension	tensile	flexibility	flexible

Task

9 Work in groups. Choose one of the following tests on parts of a bicycle: (1) the wheel, (2) the saddle, (3) the frame. Discuss how to do the test. Make notes.

10 Work individually. Use the notes from your group work. Write your description of the test under three headings.

• Objective of test   • Procedure   • Result

11 Explain your group's test to the rest of the class.

2 Resistance

Start here 1 Work in small groups. Discuss these questions.

- How do earthquakes affect high-rise buildings?
- How do you think engineers make buildings resistant to earthquakes?

Listening 2 ▶ 🎵 25 Listen to the beginning of this talk, and follow the notes. When the speaker mentions a topic in the notes, put a tick next to it.

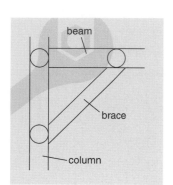

EARTHQUAKE-RESISTANT BUILDINGS

1 **Introduction: what causes earthquakes?** ✓
2 **The problem for buildings**
3 **Some solutions**
   3.1 Strengthening buildings
   3.2 Isolating buildings
   3.3 Adding dampers

---

3 Listen again and tick all the signpost phrases you hear.

Note: *signpost phrases* give directions to the listeners. They tell the listeners where they are in the talk.

Giving the purpose of the talk	Starting a new topic	Referring to visual
the main aim of this presentation is to	that brings me to	as you can see in the photo
the aim of my talk today is to	I'd like to start by	as the photo shows
my objective in this talk is to	I'd like to begin by	as shown in Figure 1
	let's move on to	the graph indicates that

4 ▶ 🎵 26 Listen to the next part of the talk and label the three diagrams which the speaker refers to. Label them Fig. 1, Fig. 2 and Fig. 3.

5 Read this key to the diagrams in 4, and write the correct diagram letters (A–F) in the blanks.

Strengthening buildings to make them earthquake-resistant

STRUCTURE 1: Single brace _____. In an earthquake, the frame of the building moves in both directions, left and right. The single diagonal is able to resist both tension and compression.

STRUCTURE 2: Cross brace _____. If two diagonals are used, they must be able to resist tension, but they do not need to be compression-resistant. This is because one diagonal is in tension when the frame moves left, while the other one is in tension when the frame moves right.

STRUCTURE 3: Horizontal deck _____. This is a flat unbendable steel plate or concrete slab. It's placed between the floors of a building. It strengthens the vertical columns and walls.

STRUCTURE 4: Horizontal truss _____. This has the same function as Structure 3, but it's located in the roof of a building. It's not a solid plate or slab. It consists of many steel triangles. It forms a rigid, unmoveable structure for the roof.

STRUCTURE 5: Rigid joint _____. This is a rigid connection between a column and a beam. In an earthquake, the connection doesn't move, but remains at right angles. The angle cannot be changed. The column and beam must be made of strong but flexible materials. They can be bent slightly, but the connection is unmoveable.

STRUCTURE 6: Shear wall _____. This is a vertical steel plate or concrete slab that can resist sideways shear forces. It forms a wall with no windows or other openings. It is usually placed around a lift shaft or stair well.

Language Here are some ways of expressing ability and inability when talking about properties:

Active: *These steel cables can resist tension. They are able to resist tension.*

Passive: *This plastic can be stretched, but it cannot be compressed.*

Some adjectives have the suffixes *-able* and *-ible* with a passive meaning, e.g. *breakable* = able to be *broken* (= you can break it); *combustible* = able to be burnt (= you can burn it).

Negative prefixes, e.g. *non-/un-/in-*: *non-portable, unbreakable, inaudible* (= it cannot be heard).

-proof: *waterproof* (= able to keep water out completely).

-resistant: *heat-resistant* (= able to withstand heat)

6 Underline examples of the above in the text in 5.

Example. The single diagonal <u>is able to resist</u> *both tension and compression.*

7 Rewrite these sentences to give the same meaning. Use **can/cannot** and the correct form of the words in brackets.

1 This plastic is heat-resistant and inflexible. (resist; bend)
2 A cross brace is resistant to tension in two directions. (withstand)
3 These sunglasses are scratchproof, but not impact-resistant. (scratch; break)
4 The emergency generator is moveable by forklift but is not portable by hand. (move; carry)

Example: 1 This plastic can resist heat and cannot be bent.

3 Results

Start here **1** Test your knowledge of safe electrical circuits. Put a tick next to the people if they get electric shocks in these situations.

(The correct answers are on page 112)

2 Work in groups. Discuss the reasons why people get (or don't get) electric shocks in the situations in 1. Explain your group's reasons to the class.

Reading **3** Read these captions. Write in the figure numbers of the diagrams they describe.

A **Fig** _____. The person gets a shock because he touches the live wire in an earthed system.

B **Fig** _____. This system is not earthed, but a tree touches the neutral wire and acts as an earth. The person touches the live wire. As a result, he gets a shock.

C **Fig** _____. There are no trees in contact, and so this system is completely unearthed. Because two people touch a wire, they both get a shock.

D **Fig** _____. The person touches the neutral wire in an earthed system, and as a result he doesn't get a shock.

E **Fig** _____. As this system is not earthed, the person can touch any wire without a shock.

F **Fig** _____. In this non-earthed system, a tree touches the live wire and acts as an earth. Two people touch a wire. One touches the neutral wire, and therefore gets a shock. The other touches the live wire. Therefore he is safe.

Language Expressing **cause**: *because, since, as*
Expressing **result** (or **effect**): *(and) so, (and) therefore, (and) as a result*

4 Replace the word(s) in italics with the word(s) in brackets. Make any necessary changes in punctuation and word order.

Example: 1 Ben touched an earthed live wire, and as a result he got a shock.

1 Ben got a shock *because* he touched an earthed live wire. (*and as a result*)

2 Ron touched an earthed neutral wire, *and as a result* he was safe. (*because*)

3 *As* Bill touched an unearthed wire, he didn't get a shock. (*and so*)

4 Bob touched a live wire when a tree touched a neutral wire. *Therefore* he got a shock. (*because*)

5 Pete touched a live wire when a tree touched it. *So* he was safe. (*since*)

6 *Since* Tom and Del touched an unearthed wire, they got a shock. (*and therefore*)

Vocabulary   A group of verbs contain the idea of cause as part of their meaning. They have the suffix *-en*, for example *strengthen* (= to cause something to be stronger).

Here is a list: *harden* (≠ *soften*), *lengthen* (≠ *shorten*), *lighten* (≠ *darken*), *strengthen* (≠ *weaken*), *tighten* (≠ *loosen*), *widen*, *flatten*, *sharpen*, *straighten*.

5 Replace the phrases in *italics* with phrases using verbs from the above list.

1 The torsion forces in the storm must have *made the bridge weaker*.
2 The purpose of adding carbon to steel is to *make it stronger*.
3 Long ago, humans used stones to *make their knife blades sharper and straighter*.
4 In forging, metal is heated to *make it softer*. Then it is put in water to *make it hard* again.
5 Hot weather *makes railway lines longer* and cold weather *makes them shorter*.
6 If the race has *made the bike saddle looser*, you should *make it tight* with a spanner.

Example. 1 The torsion forces in the storm must have weakened the bridge.

Task   **6** Work in small groups. Discuss this diagram with the rest of your group.

This is someone's theory of what might have caused the *Titanic* to sink so quickly. Do you agree with it? What else could have caused it?

7 Explain your group's opinion of the rivet theory to the rest of the class.

8 Work individually. Write an explanation of how faulty rivets could have caused the **Titanic** to sink so quickly. Use the notes and information from the diagram.

THE RIVET THEORY

WATER

● Wrought iron rivets contain slag, a by-product of iron production. This adds strength at low levels, but too much weakens the metal. Burst rivets from the *Titanic* wreck show more than three times the optimum amount.

Normal rivets **2%** slag

Titanic rivets **9%** slag

SHIP'S INTERIOR

Rivet head

Hammered end

2 inches

TITANIC RIVET

1¼ inch

1 inch

HULL PLATE

1 Rivets / Ship's interior / Hull plates / Iceberg
Plate buckles putting first rivet under strain

2 **Flawed rivet head breaks, placing extra pressure on remaining rivets**

3 **Added load causes even perfect rivets to fail, letting water in**

● Compartments at point of impact would have failed anyway, but five or six took on water. The ship could survive only four flooded compartments

A slight delay in the sinking of *Titanic* would have allowed the rescue of all the passengers by *Carpathia*

Better rivets would have saved some compartments, allowing *Titanic* to stay afloat for longer

---

Dimensions of (a) hull plates (b) rivets
Percentage of slag in iron:
  (a) normal rivets (b) *Titanic* rivets
Effect of slag on iron (strengthen? weaken?):
  at low levels? at high levels?

Cause of damage
1 iceberg hits hull → bending force on plate → shear force on rivets
2 rivet head breaks → weakens other rivets
3 extra load → good rivets break → water enters ship
4 water fills 5 or 6 compartments → ship sinks too quickly

Result: *Carpathia* too late, can't rescue passengers

Review Unit E

1 This pie chart shows the percentage of students studying different subjects in an industrial college. Describe the chart using fractions and approximations: *almost, less than, more than, just under, just over, nearly, approximately, exactly*

Begin: 1 Less than one twentieth of the students are studying software engineering.

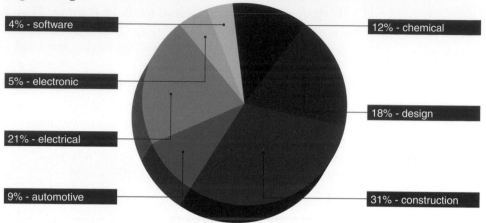

4% - software
12% - chemical
5% - electronic
18% - design
21% - electrical
9% - automotive
31% - construction

2 Match these items.

Instrument/Sensor	**What is measured/detected**
1 police lidar	a) weight
2 sound level meter	b) distance (away)
3 scales	c) distance (travelled)
4 radar	d) position
5 GPS	e) height
6 odometer	f) loudness
7 altimeter	g) speed

3 Change the direct questions into indirect questions.

1   How far has the cyclist travelled? (The odometer measures …)

_____

2   How high is the plane above sea level? (The altimeter tells the pilot …)

_____

3   How fast did the car go? (The lidar equipment told the police …)

_____

4   How heavy is the boxer? (You should use these scales to check …)

_____

5   How far were the planes from the tower? (The radar system indicated …)

_____

6   Where are the motorboats? (The GPS system will tell you exactly …)

_____

7   How loud were the guitars last night? (I used a sound level meter to find out …)

_____

Example: 1 The odometer measures how far the cyclist has travelled.

4 Change these questions into instructions. Use the verbs in brackets + **that**.

1 Are the brakes adjusted correctly? (make sure)

_____

2 Is the saddle tight and at the correct height? (check)

_____

3 Is there any lubricant on the wheel rims? (make sure/ no lubricant)

_____

4 Are the wheel spokes all at the same tension? (ensure)

_____

Example: 1 Please make sure that the brakes are adjusted correctly.

5 Fill in the gaps.

needle attached to weight

material tested

clamp

weight

The aim of the rigidity test is (1) _____ (discover/ to discover) if a material (2) _____ (deform/ deforms) or (3) _____ (breaking/breaks) when it (4) _____ (is bending/is bent) by a force. One end of the material (5) _____ (secures/is secured) in a clamp, so that the material (6) _____ (holds/is held) horizontally with one end free. A weight (7) _____ (attaches/is attached) to the free end, and then the load (8) _____ (is increased/is increasing) by adding more weights. The breaking point (9) _____ (measures/is measured). This (10) _____ (shown/shows) us the rigidity of the material.

6 Match the sentences.

1 It's flexible.
2 It's rigid.
3 It's hard.
4 It's tough.
5 It's elastic.
6 It's heat-resistant.
7 It's strong in tension.
8 It's strong in compression.
9 It has torsional strength.

a) When you heat it, it doesn't burn or deform.
b) When you drop it or strike it, it doesn't break.
c) When you compress it, it doesn't break or deform.
d) When you twist it, it doesn't break or deform.
e) You can't bend it.
f) You can bend it, and it doesn't break.
g) You can stretch it and make it longer, but it doesn't break.
h) When you pull it, it doesn't stretch or break.
i) You can't scratch it or cut it.

7 Replace the phrases in italics with phrases using **make/made** + comparative adjective.

1 We need to bring some diggers here *to deepen the trench*.

_____

2 Last year's small earthquakes have *weakened the foundations*.

_____

3 The only way to *strengthen the walls* is to add braces between them.

_____

4 You have to *soften the metal* before you can hammer it into shape.

_____

Example: 1 We need to bring some diggers here to make the trench deeper.

8 Work in groups. Discuss these questions about the three car tests below.

- What is the purpose of each test?
- Which parts of the car are tested?
- What properties are tested?
- What is the procedure for each test? How is each test done?
- What measurements are made after the test?
- How does a car pass the test? What is a good result for the car?
- If a car fails a test, what would you recommend?

FRAME TEST

Average weight of a car:	1440 kg
Average weight of the plate:	2120 kg (50% more than car)

TEST RESULT:

the roof must not bend more than 12.5 cm

DROP TEST

1.5 m

ROLL TEST

Truck (30 mph)

23°

9 Work individually. Use the notes from your group work. Write a description of the three tests, including this information

- the objectives of each test
- how to carry out each test
- how to pass each test

10 Here are the results of a new car model (the Sunburst XJ22) in the three tests. Write a short report.

- explain the results of each test
- make recommendations

NEW MODEL TESTED	Sunburst XJ22
TEST RESULTS	
FRAME TEST	roof bent 3.2 cm
DROP TEST	roof bent 12.8 cm
ROLL TEST	dummy was thrown 2.2 m from car

11 Work in small groups. Choose one of the events below, and discuss these questions.

- What caused the event?
- What was the result of the event?
- How can the event be prevented or managed? What actions should be taken?

Events

1 The Columbia shuttle disaster (2003)
2 Loss of the Ariane 5 super rocket (2003)
3 The Indian Ocean Tsunami (2004)

1. Launch:
16 Jan 2003
Foam from external tank strikes wing

2. Attempted re-entry:
1 Feb 2003
Crack in leading edge caused by impact allows superheated gas to penetrate. Wing interior melts and disintegrates

Solid rocket boosters

Landing gear

External fuel tank

1 2221 GMT Ariane 5 takes off from Kourou

2 2223 Solid fuel boosters separate

3 2224 Rocket fails to achieve desired height and speed

4 2225 Self destruct mechanism destroys rocket

5 Two satellites are lost at sea

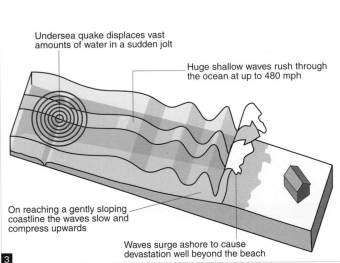

Undersea quake displaces vast amounts of water in a sudden jolt

Huge shallow waves rush through the ocean at up to 480 mph

On reaching a gently sloping coastline the waves slow and compress upwards

Waves surge ashore to cause devastation well beyond the beach

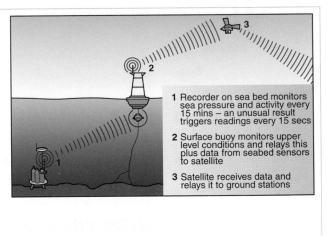

1 Recorder on sea bed monitors sea pressure and activity every 15 mins – an unusual result triggers readings every 15 secs

2 Surface buoy monitors upper level conditions and relays this plus data from seabed sensors to satellite

3 Satellite receives data and relays it to ground stations

The world's biggest quake in 40 years unleashed walls of water that devastated coastlines around the Indian Ocean

12 Report your group's ideas to the class. Answer their questions.

Project **13** Find out about an important test in your industry. Get information about

- the objectives of the test
- the test procedure
- results

14 Give a short talk about this to the class.

1 Working robots

Start here **1** Brainstorm with a partner. What kind of working robots have you heard about? What jobs do they do?

Scanning **2** Practise your speed reading. Look for the information you need on the SPEED SEARCH pages (118–119). Try to be the first to complete the task.

Task: Answer these questions about robots.
- What percentage of the world's robots work in car assembly?
- Which country has about half of the world's robots?
- How far have the Mars robots *Spirit* and *Opportunity* travelled on Mars?

Listening **3** Look at these robots. What do you think they do?

4 **27** Listen to these interviews with participants at an industrial robot convention. Which robots (in 3) are the speakers talking about?

5 Listen again. Each participant mentions some strengths and weaknesses of the robots, and suggests some improvements. Complete the form.

ROBOT USER SURVEY FORM

USER # 1	OCCUPATION: Construction engineer		ROBOT NAME: Snakebot
Function of robot	It brings		
Strength(s)	1.	2.	
Weakness(es)			
Improvement(s)			

USER # 2	OCCUPATION: Emergency response		ROBOT NAME: Rescue Robot
Function of robot			
Strength(s)	1.	2.	
Weakness(es)			
Improvement(s)			

6 ▶ 🔊 **28** Listen to part of the first interview again. Complete this transcript with the correct form of the words in the box.

advantage disadvantage drawback suggest could
should that strength weakness would

I: *So what are the* (1) *advantages of the SnakeBot?*
P1: Well, its main (2) _____ is that it can twist around things like girders, pipes and scaffolding.
I: *Excellent. So, would you say that it has any* (3) _____, *or* (4) _____?
P1: *Yes, its main* (5) _____ *is* (6) _____ *you have to control every movement with a joystick.*
I: So, in the future, how (7) _____ you (8) _____ that it (9) _____ be improved?
P1: *Well, I* (10) _____ *suggest* (11) _____ *you* (12) _____ *design a voice-activated SnakeBot.*

Speaking **7** Tell the class about the strengths and weaknesses of some of these products and/or any others you have problems with. Suggest improvements.

computer keyboard, MP3 player, earphones, sunglasses, mobile phone, digital camera, TV remote

8 Work in pairs, A and B.

Student A.
1 You are conducting a survey of people who use robots in their work. Ask B about their robot and make notes in the form.
2 Turn to page 113 for information about you and your robot. Answer B's questions.

Student B.
1 Turn to page 116 for information about you and your robot. Answer A's questions.
2 You are conducting a survey of people who use robots in their work. Ask A about their robot and make notes in the form.

ROBOT USER SURVEY	
Occupation of user	
Name of robot	
Function of robot	
Frequency of use	
Specifications of robot	
How it works	
Strength(s)	
Weakness(es)	
Suggested improvement(s)	

Writing **9** Write a short report about your partner's robot and how it could be improved. Use the information from the form.

2 Eco-friendly planes

Start here **1** What do you know about the forces which act on a plane?

- Label the diagram with these words: *thrust*, *weight*, *drag*, *lift*.
- Explain the role of *the engine*, *gravity*, *friction* and *shape of wing* in these forces.

Reading **2** Read this magazine article and write the plane design numbers in the gaps.

Design A

engine

fuselage

Design B

airflow

inlet

Design C

Design D

Eco-friendly
PLANES
of the future

Here are four designs for future passenger planes. The aim of all the designs is to reduce drag (or friction of the wing against the air). As a result, they will all consume less fuel, and cause less damage to the environment.

In **Design** _____, the rear of the fuselage doesn't taper to a point. Instead, it's a cone with curved sides and a flat top (not a point), shaped like a lampshade. Between the cone and the engine there is an intake port which goes around the whole fuselage like a ring. Here a fan sucks in air and expels it from the end of the cone. This design makes the air flow smoothly across the rear of the fuselage, and reduces friction. As a result, the plane needs three-fifths less engine thrust, and the fuel consumption is one-fifth lower.

Design _____ uses diagonal struts (or braces) to support the aircraft's wings. On each side of the plane, there are diagonal struts from the tail and fuselage to the wingtips. These strengthen the wings. As a result, wings can be longer, stronger but much lighter. This means that the wings weigh two-thirds less than normal wings, which reduces wing drag. The result is that the engine needs 20% less thrust than today's plane engines, and the fuel consumption is one quarter less.

Design _____ re-uses a technology from the past: propellers. A jet turbine drives specially-shaped propellers that make the air flow smoothly and reduce wing drag. Although this type of engine is slower (with a top speed of 675 km per hour) and noisier than today's jet engines, it consumes much less fuel (almost a third less). This plane will perform best on shorter flights of less than 3000 km.

Design _____ combines the wings and fuselage into a single triangular structure. Three engines are placed at the rear, and the wingtips are bent upwards. As a result, the drag and engine thrust are over one-tenth lower than in today's planes, and fuel consumption is a quarter less. One disadvantage of this design is that the fuselage is flat, not cylindrical, and so it may not resist air pressure at high altitudes. But an important advantage is that the plane is much quieter than today's planes.

3 The designers of the new planes in 2 worked from the design brief below. Discuss with your partner and choose:

- the best design (the one closest to the design brief)
- the worst design (the one furthest from the design brief)

DESIGN BRIEF FOR NEW PASSENGER PLANE

1 The need

Environmental issues are very important today. Global warming and non-renewable energy resources are major problems. It is necessary to design aeroplanes which will (a) use less fuel and (b) emit less greenhouse gas into the atmosphere. In addition, (c) noise pollution has to be reduced.

2 Problems with current designs

Aeroplanes today have a number of design weaknesses. The shape of wings and fuselages create friction (or drag), so that air does not flow smoothly over them. In addition, wings have to be strong, and as a result they are very heavy. This results in more engine thrust, more fuel consumption and more carbon emissions. Another problem is that engine noise is high.

3 Requirements for new design

Design a new plane which will consume at least 20% less fuel. The shape and design of the new wing and/or fuselage needs to allow air to flow more smoothly. As a result, engine thrust and drag must be reduced by at least 10%. The wingspan should be longer, but fewer materials must be used and the wing must be lighter than current planes. The shape of the fuselage can be changed, but it must remain cylindrical and pressure-resistant for passenger safety. Current noise levels must not be increased.

Task **4** Work in small groups. Follow your group's design brief to design an improved product. Draw a diagram and write a description. Include this information. You can add more features.

- function
- shape and appearance
- main parts
- dimensions
- materials and properties
- operation (how it works)
- cost
- method of manufacture
- safety features

Group A. Your design brief is on page 111.
Group B. Your design brief is on page 113.
Group C. Your design brief is on page 114.
Group D. Your design brief is on page 116.

5 Present your new design to the class.

6 Listen to the presentations by the other group(s).

- Does their design meet the brief? Tell them why/why not.
- Tell them the advantages and disadvantages of their design.

3 Free-flying sails

Start here **1** What problems does this design help to solve?

Listening **2** ▶ 🎵 29 Listen to this designer giving a presentation about the traction kite. Put her index card notes into the correct order by numbering them 1–12.

capsule (for crew and computers)

A

Materials and properties

Kite: made of polyester.
Properties: tough, flexible, lightweight, high tensile strength, low friction.

☐

B

Advantages

Wind power a renewable source.
Ships use 35% less fuel on voyage.
Carbon emissions are reduced.
Less expensive for ship owners.

☐

C

Problem

Other designs use mast and sail fixed permanently to a ship. This is very expensive.

☐

D

The kite catches the wind.
Kite pulls ship with 6000 hp.
When wind direction changes, kite is untied from ship and travels to another client ship.

☐

E

Parts and functions

Kite has two large sails.
Sails attached to large oval balloon.
Balloon filled with helium.

☐

F

Operation

Kite crew steer kite to client ship.
They drop cable down to ship.
Ship's crew attach cable to front of ship.

☐

G

Sensors on sails detect air pressure and air speed, and send data to the computers. Computers control speed and direction.
Kite connected to client ship using strong cable.

☐

H

Need

Cargo ships weigh tens of thousands of tons.
Diesel oil non-renewable and expensive.
Need to use less oil, therefore use wind energy by means of sails.

☐

I

Design brief

To design a traction kite
(a) strong enough to pull a large cargo ship through water and
(b) removeable from ship when there is no wind.

☐

J

Greet audience (don't forget!)

Objective of presentation
To tell audience about new traction kite for cargo ships and supertankers.

☐

K

Small capsule suspended from balloon. Capsule contains a 3-man crew and computers.

☐

L

Dimensions

Wingspan: 120 m.
Area of sail: 5000 m².
Altitude: 300 m above sea level.

☐

3 The speaker introduces each section using signpost phrases and questions. Complete the phrases. Use the words in the box once only.

| aim | brings | finally | let's | mention | move | need | problem | start | talk | turn |

Speaker's headings	Speaker's words
Greeting	Good morning everyone, and thanks for coming.
Objective	Signpost: The (1) _____ of this short presentation is to tell you about our new traction kite.
Need	Signpost: I'd like to (2) _____ by asking a question. Question: *Why do we (3) _____ a traction kite?*
Problem	Question: *So what is the (4) _____ with other designs for sails?*
Design brief	Signpost: And that (5) _____ me to our design brief.
Materials and properties	Signpost: Now let's (6) _____ on to materials. Question: *What is the traction kite made of?* Question: *And what are the properties of the materials?*
Parts and functions	Signpost: Right, so now (7) _____ look at the main parts of the traction kite, and their function.
Dimensions	Question: *So how large is this kite?* Question: *And how high does it fly?* Signpost: Let's (8) _____ at some dimensions.
Operation	Signpost: All right, now let's (9) _____ to the operation of the kite. Question: *How does it work?*
Advantages	Signpost: And (10) _____, I'd like to (11) _____ some of the advantages of the traction kite.

4 Listen again to the presentation. Check your answers to 3.

Speaking **5** Make short presentations based on these sets of notes. Use signpost phrases or questions to signal when you move to the next point.

GREETING

AIM: *describe MP3 player 4 GB*

SIZE AND WEIGHT: *90 x 40 x 6. 85 mm; display 38.1 mm; weight 0.0425 g*

MATERIALS: *stainless steel body; polymer display*

CONTROLS: *click wheel; centre button; headphone port; USB port*

OPERATION: *insert earphone jack in socket; press menu on click wheel; scroll to tune; select tune; click centre button*

ACCESSORIES: *headphones, USB connector, leather or plastic cover, belt attachment*

THANKS

GREETING

OBJECTIVE: talk about ePhone

TECHNOLOGY: multi-touch display; QWERTY soft keyboard

FUNCTION: ePhone is multi-functional:
(1) media player; (2) mobile phone;
(3) internet

(1) MEDIA FEATURES: wide 88.9 mm touchscreen for music, video, TV shows, films

(2) PHONE FEATURES: name or number on screen, and click; voicemail; camera

(3) INTERNET FEATURES: email and web browser; transfers bookmarks from PC/Mac; built-in Google and Yahoo! search

THANKS

Innovation

1 Zero emission

Start here

1 Work with a partner. Discuss these questions.

- What are *zero-emission* cars?
- How do they help the environment?
- What technology do they use?

2 How do you think this car works? Discuss with your partner.

fuel cell   ultra-capacitor

drive motor
Fig. 1 Idling

Fig. 2 Braking

fuel cell   ultra-capacitor

drive motor
Fig. 3 Starting

Fig. 4 Cruising

Task

3 The inventors of the above car combined two different technologies – fuel cells and capacitors – to invent a new power system. Work in pairs. Find out about them.

Student A. Find out about hydrogen fuel cells on page 115.

Student B. Find out about capacitors on page 117.

4 Explain to your partner how your technology works.

5 Join up with other pairs to work in small groups. Decide how the inventors combined the two technologies together to produce the car in 2.

6 Explain your group's ideas to the class.

Writing

7 You are a TV journalist. You are going to interview one of the inventors of the Hydro-X car using these notes. Write questions to ask the inventor.

New type of car needed? Why? To protect environment?
Problems with current cars? Petrol/diesel engines? Other hydrogen fuel cell cars?
New Hydro-X car … Maximum speed (km/h)? Range (km)? Acceleration? Emissions?
Hydro-X based on … what technology?
Advantages of new Hydro-X?
Components … *Fuel cell* … Power output (kW)? Location (front/rear/underneath)? Why located there?
Motor … Location? Output (kW)?
Control unit … Function/Purpose?
Ultra-capacitor … Function? Location? Why located there?
Hydrogen storage tanks … Location? Capacity (L/kg)? How connected to fuel cell?
Air pump … Why needed?
Operation – how the Hydro-X works … Starting? Cruising? Braking? Idling?

Reading   **8**   Read the press release and find answers to the questions you have written.

The new Hydro-X hydrogen fuel cell car – information for the news media

Need The environment needs to be protected. Consumption of fossil fuel has to fall. Emissions of greenhouse gases (carbon dioxide, nitrous oxide, and methane) into the atmosphere must be reduced.

Problems Petrol and diesel engines consume too much fossil fuel and emit too much greenhouse gas. Hydrogen fuel cells solve this problem, but they are usually too heavy and have low acceleration.

Solution The new Hydro-X is a car with a lightweight hydrogen fuel cell. It can accelerate quickly and cruise at high speeds of 160 km/h. It has a range of 480 km. Its only emission is water vapour.

Technology The car is based on two technologies: the hydrogen fuel cell and the ultra-capacitor. An ultra-capacitor is a powerful capacitor which provides enough output for fast acceleration.

Advantages The fuel cell in this vehicle is smaller and lighter than the ones used in other vehicles, because it's not needed for acceleration. As a result, the vehicle is lighter. However, it's also more powerful because of the ultra-capacitors.

Components The *fuel cell*, positioned under the floor to provide more space, provides a maximum output of 93 kW. The *motor*, mounted between the front wheels, provides high output (90 kW) and powerful torque (276 Nm). The *control unit*, located over the motor, controls the electrical systems. The *ultra-capacitor*, set at an angle behind the rear seat to increase luggage space, delivers immediate high-output power during startup and acceleration, and recovers energy generated during braking. The *hydrogen storage tanks*, placed under the rear seat, can be filled with 168.3 L of compressed hydrogen gas. They're connected to the fuel cell by special pipes. The *air pump*, mounted directly on the motor, supplies the fuel cell with oxygen.

Operation There are four stages. *1 Acceleration*. Power comes from both the ultra-capacitor and the fuel cell to provide powerful acceleration (See Fig _____). *2 Steady speed*. Power comes from the fuel cell, but not from the capacitor (See Fig _____). *3 Deceleration*. The ultra-capacitor absorbs the energy released during deceleration and stores it with power from the fuel cell (See Fig _____). *4 Stopped*. There is no power from the fuel cell. The electricity needed to operate the air conditioner and other components is supplied by the ultra-capacitor. (See Fig _____).

   9   The figure numbers are missing from the final paragraph in 8. Fill in the gaps. Refer to the diagrams in 2.

Speaking   **10**   Roleplay the interview between the journalist and the inventor.

Language   These sentences mean the same. The words in the box can be omitted to keep the same meaning.

- *The ultra-capacitor recovers the energy* which is *released during deceleration.*
- *The ultra-capacitor recovers the energy released during deceleration.*

The words in blue are an example of a reduced relative clause.

   11   Underline the reduced relative clauses in these sentences.

1 The Hydro-X fuel cell is lighter than the ones <u>used in other vehicles</u>.
2 The fuel cell, positioned under the floor, provides an output of 93 kW.
3 The motor, located between the front wheels, provides a powerful torque.
4 The fuel tanks, placed under the rear seat, are filled with hydrogen.
5 The ultra-capacitor absorbs the energy released during braking.
6 The electricity needed to operate the lights comes from the ultra-capacitor.

   12   Insert one of these phrases where possible in each sentence above, and in eight places in 8.

which is, which are

2 Technological change

Start here **1** Work in pairs. What are the 10 most important tools in the history of mankind? Make a list and put them in order of importance.

Note: the tools must be *hand-held* or *easily portable*. Do not include *simple machines* (such as levers or pulleys), *heavy machine tools* (like hydraulic jacks) or *complex*, *self-running machines* (such as cars, windmills or computers).

2 Explain your list to the class. Give reasons for your group's choice.

3 Compare your list with the results of a survey on page 111. Do you agree with their list? Give reasons.

Reading **4** Read this magazine article and mark the inventions on the timeline.

Note: a century ends in its own number. The 14th century is 1301–1400.

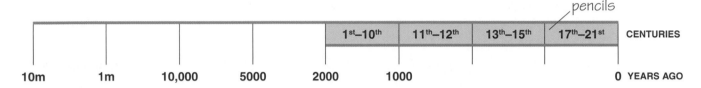

Tools through the ages

THE FIRST KNIVES were made about two and a half million years ago. They were crafted by early ancestors of modern humans. At first, sharp pieces of stone were broken off a rock, but in later times they were sharpened and straightened into blades.

The abacus is one of the first mechanical counting devices, an ancestor of today's computers. It consisted of a frame containing beads on wires. The modern abacus was designed by the Chinese around the year 1200.

The compass allowed sailors to navigate across oceans and discover new worlds. The compass was invented by the Chinese about 2200 years ago. A spoon-shaped piece of magnetic rock was balanced on a flat surface. Since it was magnetic, the handle rotated to align itself with the Earth's magnetic poles.

The first mass-produced pencils were made in Germany in 1662, which helped writing and education to develop.

The harness lets people control horses and attach them to carts. It was probably invented about 6000 years ago, when horses were first tamed and kept.

The scythe allows people to cut grass and harvest crops from the field. It consists of a long wooden shaft with handles on the end and in the middle, and a long curved blade on the other end. The blade is sharp on the inside. It was first used in Europe in the 12th century.

Glasses (or spectacles) make workers more productive and accurate, and allow people to work into old age. Mathematical calculations for a spherical lens were first made by Arab scientists in the 11th century. The first spectacles were manufactured by Italian craftsmen in the 13th century.

Saws were first used by the Egyptians more than 5000 years ago to cut both wood and stone. They were made of copper.

The first balance scales were seen in southern Mesopotamia about 9000 years ago. They consisted of two weighing pans attached to either end of a beam, which was balanced on a central pivot. They allowed merchants to calculate the exact weight of goods.

The chisel consists of a long, narrow, sharpened edge attached to a handle. It's different from a knife or axe, because it is driven by a sharp blow from a hammer or mallet. The earliest chisels were made from flint (a kind of stone) 10,000 years ago. Later, they were used by the Egyptians to carve stone for the pyramids.

Vocabulary **5** Do you know these simple machines? Match the pictures with the words and phrases in the box.

| cam and follower   crank and rod   gear   lever   pulley and belt   rack and pinion |
| ratchet and pawl   screw   wheel and axle   wedge |

(Answers on page 114)

6 Which of these simple machines are used in your industry or technical field? How are they used? Explain to the class.

Language **7** Complete this article about the history of oil drilling. Use the correct form (present or past, active or passive) of the verbs in brackets.

Drilling for oil – past and present

Long ago, wells (1) <u>were dug</u> (dig) in the ground using percussion drilling. A heavy wooden cutting tool (2) _____ (suspend) by a rope from a pulley on a wooden tripod. The tool (3) _____ (pull up) by hand or steam engine, and then it (4) _____ (drop) into the hole. The rock (5) _____ (break) by the weight of the tool. The maximum depth was only about 70 metres.

Nowadays, much deeper oil wells of 700 m (6) _____ (dig) using a method called rotary drilling. A sharp drill bit (7) _____ (suspend) by a drill string from a pulley on a steel derrick. The drill bit (8) _____ (rotate) in the hole by a powerful engine. The rock (9) _____ (break) by the rotation of the drill bit.

Now there is also a new method of drilling which (10) <u>cuts</u> (cut) the rock using lasers. No cutting tool or drill bit (11) _____ (use). Instead, the rock (12) _____ (split) by beams of high-energy light. A fibre-optic cable (13) _____ (carry) the light from the lasers on the surface down the hole to a set of lenses. The lenses then (14) _____ (focus) the light to a sharp point on the rock face, which (15) _____ (cut) almost 100 times faster than by a drill bit. As a result, the cost of drilling (16) _____ (reduce), and drilling jobs (17) _____ (complete) much more quickly.

Task **8** Work in small groups.

- Choose an industry or work process which you know something about. *Examples: building, heavy lifting, fishing, mining, road-building, communications, sea or land travel, heating, lighting, pumping, irrigation*
- How was the work done in the past? How is it done now? Make notes showing the contrast between past and present.
- Explain your group's ideas to the class.

3 Vehicle safety

Start here

1 What car safety systems are new cars fitted with? Make a list of the latest safety devices. Compare it with a partner's list.

2 How do you think the safety systems on the right work? Discuss with your partner.

Listening

3 ▶ 🔘 **30** Listen to this interview between a radio journalist and an expert on car safety systems. Which system from 2 are they discussing?

4 Listen to the interview again. As you listen, look at the journalist's checklist. Delete any questions she does not ask.

1   Side Impact Protection System

2   Smart Adaptive Cruise Control

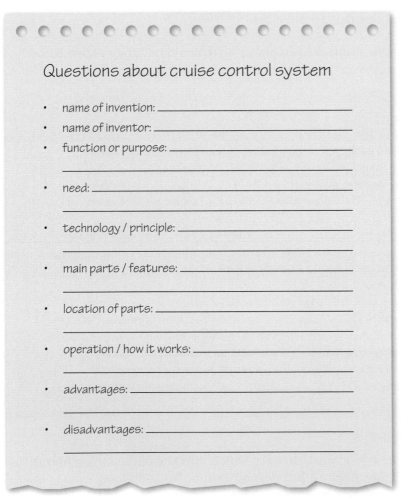

Questions about cruise control system

- name of invention: _____
- name of inventor: _____
- function or purpose: _____
  _____
- need: _____
  _____
- technology / principle: _____
  _____
- main parts / features: _____
  _____
- location of parts: _____
  _____
- operation / how it works: _____
  _____
- advantages: _____
  _____
- disadvantages: _____
  _____

3   Rear Obstacle Warning System

5 Listen to the interview again and note down the main points of the expert's answers in the checklist.

Listening   **6**   ▶ 💿 31   The journalist is interviewing the car safety engineer about her career. Correct the mistakes in her biodata.

Michela Rossi is 24, a design engineer at Central Motors. She gained her technician's diploma in automotive manufacture from Toulouse Technical Institute and then a gained a degree in automotive engineering at the Polytechnic University of Turin. She joined Central Motors four years ago, and in that time she has designed or invented four new products with her team. She's now working on a new type of air bag for cars. She plans to continue working in Central Motors for several years and then she wants to start her own design company.

Speaking   **7**   Work in pairs, A and B. Roleplay an interview between a journalist and a car safety engineer.

Student A: You are the radio journalist. Interview Student B about his/her career. Find out about B's *age, company, how long in company, job title, number of inventions, diploma, degree, plans for future inventions, plans for career.*

Student B: You are a car safety engineer. You can use one of the bio-data fact sheets on page 117. Alternatively, you can make some notes using similar information about yourself. Answer A's questions.

8   Find out about each other's car safety system. Take turns to roleplay the parts of a journalist and a car safety expert.

Student A: You are an expert on the Side Impact Protection System (SIPS). Read the factsheet on page 114 and refer to the diagram in 2. Answer a journalist's questions about the SIPS system.

Student B: You are an expert on the Rear Obstacle Warning System (ROWS). Read the fact sheet on page 117 and refer to the diagram in 2. Answer a journalist's questions about the ROWS system.

Writing   **9**   Write a press release on your car safety system. Refer to the press release on page 91. Use these headings.

Need for this safety system	Main components
Problems with current systems	Location of each component
Description of new system	Function of each component
Technology used in system	How the system works
Advantages	

Task   **10**   Work in small groups.

- Choose one of the car systems on pages 113, 115 or 116.
- Read the fact sheet. Add notes giving your own ideas and opinions about the system.
- Explain the system to the rest of the group.
- Answer their questions about it.

1 Write questions to get the answers in the questionnaire below.

Q 6 How _____?

Q 8 When _____?

Q 10 Are _____?

Q 11 What _____?

Q 12 What _____?

Q 13 Where _____?

Q 16 How _____?

Q 17 What _____?

Q 18 Does _____?

Q 19 How _____?

2 Work in pairs. Practise the interview. Use the questionnaire.

ROBOT USER SURVEY

1 **Age:** 18–21 ☐   22–30 ☒   31–45 ☐   > 46 ☐

2 **Job type:** operative ☐   technician ☒   engineer ☐   manager ☐   other _____

3 **Exact job title:** Building Safety inspector

4 **Workplace:** factory ☐   office ☐   site ☒   laboratory ☐   other _____

5 **Industry:** construction ☒   electrical ☐   telecom ☐   IT ☐   biomed ☐   other _____

6 **No of years in job:** < 5 ☒   5–10 ☐   11–20 ☐   > 20 ☐

7 **Type of robot used:** Robo Inspector

8 **Date of purchase:** 8 months ago.

9 **Frequency of use:** < 10% ☐   10–25% ☐   26–50% ☐   51–75% ☒   > 75% ☐

10 **Using now/today?** YES ☒   NO ☐

11 **Main function/purpose:** moving ☐   detecting ☒   doing ☐   other _____

12 **Abilities:** walk ☐   run ☐   ride ☐   carry ☒   other climb

13 **Location of use:** On buildings

14 **Shape:** Triangular with 3 wheels. Flat.

15 **Approximate dimensions:** 27cm x 6cm

16 **Method of operation:** Battery-operated remote control.

17 **Advantages/strengths:** Can go up dangerous walls.

18 **Disadvantages/weaknesses/design flaws:** They crash into each other.

19 **Suggested improvements:** Add tracking sensors to them.

20 **Comparison with human: better** ☒   **worse** ☐

3 Match each signpost with the information which follows it.

Signpost	Information
1 First I'd like to give you a definition of the SnakeBot. 2 OK, I've defined the device. But what is it able to do? 3 Now let's move on to the main components of the robot. 4 Right, now I'd like to talk about the function of each component. 5 OK, we've looked at its parts and what they do, so now let's look at its operation. 6 And finally, I'd like to mention its main strengths.	a) There are about 30 modules in the SnakeBot, and they're all linked together by rods and wires. Every module has a micro-computer in it. This is connected to sensors, motors, wheels and gears. The SnakeBot's head holds the main computer. b) A SnakeBot is basically a computer-controlled robotic device which looks and moves like a snake. c) It works like this. The controller moves a joystick to tell the SnakeBot where to go. The main computer picks up this message wirelessly and then 'tells' the microcontrollers what to do. At the same time, the sensors 'feel' the surface, and send this data to the microcontrollers. These controllers make the gears, wheels and rods move. d) The most important advantage of the SnakeBot is that you can control it remotely from a long distance. e) It can climb scaffolding and carry a tool to a builder at the top of a high-rise building. f) The job of the main computer is to control the other modules. The sensors also have an important job to do. They detect changes in the ground and send this data to the micro-computers.

4 Complete this set of notes using a device you know about.

Aim: to talk about	(name of device)
Specifications:	(e.g. dimensions, weight, speed)
Main parts and functions:	
Materials and properties:	
Operation/How it works:	
Strengths:	
Weaknesses:	

5 Give a short talk from your notes. Use signpost phrases or questions to signal when you move to the next point in the notes.

Remember to begin your talk by welcoming the audience, and end by thanking them.

6 Complete this text. Use the present or past passive of the verbs in brackets.

Here are some examples of spinoffs from space travel. The devices (1) _were created_ (create) many years ago for space programmes. But now they (2) _are used_ (use) by many people in everyday life.

The smoke detector (3) _____ (make) for the Skylab space station in the 1970s to detect toxic gases. Now they (4) _____ (install) in most buildings to warn people of fire.

The CADCAM computer program (5) _____ (invent) by NASA engineers over 20 years ago to find problems in spaceships. Now nearly all cars (6) _____ (design) using these programs.

Today many computer games (7) _____ (control) by means of small joysticks. In fact joysticks (8) _____ (introduce) many years ago to control the Apollo Lunar Rover.

7 Write a description of the space elevator, using all the information. Add your own ideas and opinions.

You can use your own headings to paragraphs, or use these words in your headings: *definition, purpose, main components, function of components, specifications, dimensions, location, speed, material, properties, operation, advantages, problems.*

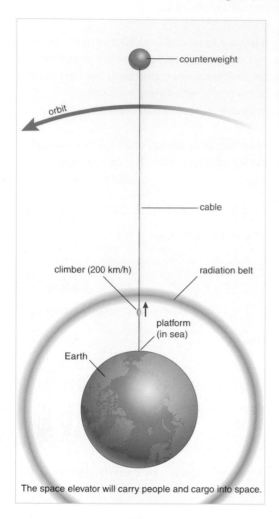

The space elevator will carry people and cargo into space.

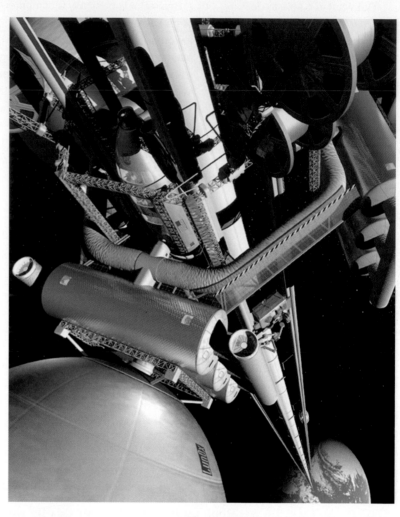

CABLE FOR SPACE ELEVATOR	
length	100,000 km
material	carbon nanotubes
properties	light, cheap, strong in tension
advantage	can manufacture it cheaply

Advantage: rocket propulsion not needed
Problem: radiation belt at 1000–20,000 km altitude

Operation

counterweight floats in zero gravity

earth rotates → platform pulls cable → counterweight tightens it

robot climber moves up cable, escapes gravity of Earth

8 Insert one of the phrases from the box in the text where possible. Use each phrase once only.

> that are   that is   which is   which was

> Smart Adaptive Cruise Control is a car safety system invented by a team of engineers at Central Motors. It can be found in all new cars manufactured by Central Motors. It is an automatic impact-prevention system, designed to maintain a safe distance between your car and the vehicle in front. It uses a laser sensor mounted on the front of the vehicle in the upper part of the windscreen.

9 Work with a partner. Discuss these inventions.

- What need or problem do they attempt to solve?
- What is their purpose? (Answers on page 116)
- What are their strengths and weaknesses?

Project **10** Work individually.

- Research the history of a key technology in your industry.
- Draw a timeline with notes of important changes in the technology.
- Write notes about the past, present and future of the technology.
- Prepare and give a short talk to the class.

11 Work in small groups.

- Choose a product that you would like to improve or re-design.
- Use the internet and/or a library to find ideas for a new design.
- Brainstorm ways to modify and improve the product. Make notes.
- Using your notes, discuss and decide the design brief.
- Write the design brief for the new product.
- Design the new product, following your group's design brief. Make sketches.
- Prepare a presentation about your new product. Draw a large visual to show the class.
- Give a group presentation about your new product. Refer to your visual during your talk.

Grammar summary

A Grammar

Present simple

Positive		
He/She	works/studies	at Oxford University.
I/You/We/They	work/study	
The water	flows	into the tank.
The electrons	flow	along the wire.

Negative				
I/We/They	do	not	work	on an oil platform.
He/She	does			

Question			
Where	do	you/they	work?
	does	he/she	

The present simple is used to talk about
(1) regular or routine events: *Tore goes home to Norway every four weeks.*
(2) job descriptions: *The chief electrician supervises a team of four electricians.*
(3) processes: *The water flows from the tank into the solar water panel.*

Present continuous

Positive			
I	am	studying	electronics.
You/We/They	are	breaking	the safety rules.
He/She/The robot	is	cleaning	the car.

Negative				
I	am	not	studying	electronics.
You/We/They	are	not	breaking	the safety rules.
He/She/The robot	is	not	cleaning	the car.

Question			
Am	I	talking	to the manager?
Are	you/we/they	working	on the same project?
Is	he/she/the robot	wearing	a hard hat?

The present continuous is used to talk about
(1) things happening now (while the speaker is speaking): *I'm taking the wheel off now.*
(2) things happening for a limited time around now: *I'm studying electronics this year.*
(3) plans or intentions for the near future: *I'm flying home tomorrow.*

Future

will and *won't* are used to talk about things that you think are certain to happen in the future.
I won't be at the meeting. I'll be in Paris all next week. The train from London will arrive at platform 2.
The present continuous or *going to* + verb is used to talk about plans or intentions.
I'm holding a meeting next Thursday. I'm going to hold a meeting next Thursday.
to is used after verbs such as *plan, intend, want, hope.*
I want to finish this report next week. I intend to complete this project next month. I hope to do it tomorrow.

Present perfect

The present perfect uses *have/has* + past participle.

Positive			
I/You/We/They	have	repaired	the car.
He/She	has	broken	the printer.

Negative				
I/You/We/They	have	not	repaired	the car.
He/She	has	not	broken	the printer.

Question			
Have	you/they	repaired	the car?
Has	he/she	broken	the printer?

The present perfect is used to talk about events during a period of time lasting from the past right up to the present time.

You can use *for, since, just* and *yet*:

- *for* focusses on the length of a period of time: *Jan has worked in Britain for three years.* (Jan is still working in Britain.)
- *since* focusses on the starting point of a period of time: *Jan has worked in Britain since 2008.* (Jan is still working in Britain.)
- *just* emphasises that the event happened recently: *My car has just broken down.* (This happened perhaps one or two minutes before now).
- *yet* (in questions and negatives) emphasises the period of time to the present. *Haven't you finished that job yet? He hasn't cleaned the car yet.* (The job is not done. The car is dirty.)

The present perfect isn't used with times or dates of the event.

Past simple

Positive			
I/You/We/They	repaired	the car	yesterday.
He/She/It	broke	the printer	two days ago.

Negative					
I/You/We/They	did	not	repair	the car	yesterday.
He/She/It			break	the printer	two days ago.

Question				
When	did	I/you/we/they/he/she/it	repair	the car?
			break	the printer?

The past simple is used to talk about events which happened at a specific time in the past.

You can use these time expressions with the past simple:
- *yesterday, this morning, the day before yesterday*
- *three minutes ago, two days ago, five weeks ago*
- *last week, last month, last year*
- *in 2005, on the 20th October, at 6.30*

Present perfect v past simple
Here is an example of the difference between the present perfect and the past simple. Anna has written this in her CV:

Work experience 1
Dates September 2006 to the present day
Employer Omega Studios

September 2006 to the present day is a period of time from the past to the present. Anna still works in Omega Studios, and so these questions and answers use the present perfect:

Q: *How long have you worked at Omega Studios?*
A: *I've worked at Omega from 2006 to the present day. I've worked there since 2006. I've been there for two/three/ten years.*

Anna has also written this:

Work experience 2
Dates 2003–2005
Employer Comet Electronics

2003–2005 is a period of time in the past, and so these questions and answers use the past simple:

Q: *How long did you work at Comet Electronics?*
A: *I worked at Comet from 2003 to 2005. I worked there for two years.*
Q: *When did you join the company?*
A: *I joined it in July 2003. I started there four/five/ten years ago.*

The pronoun *one*
one is used when
- someone has already mentioned a thing,
- there is a choice between two or more types of the thing, and
- you don't want to repeat the name of the thing.

A: *Please pass me a spanner.*
B: *Which one do you want? The long one or the short one?*

Speaker B mentions two types of spanner, but does not want to repeat the word *spanner*.

Here are some common combinations:

Which one? Which ones? This one. These ones. That one. Those ones. The red one. The other one. The one with the cover. The one without the handle.

Present simple passive

In an active sentence, the subject is the same as the agent. The subject does the action.

Subject = Agent	Active verb	Object
400 robots	paint	the car body.
Five technicians	service	the robots.

In a passive sentence, the subject is NOT the same as the agent. The subject doesn't do the action. The agent does the action to the subject.

Subject	Passive verb		Agent
	be	Past participle	
The car body	is	painted	by 400 robots.
The robots	are	serviced	by five technicians.

The passive is often used in technical writing for two main reasons:

1 The passive can make the writing clearer:

The water flows into the radiator. (ACTIVE)
Here the fan cools it. (ACTIVE)
➔ *The water flows into the radiator.* (ACTIVE*)*.
Here it is cooled by the fan. (PASSIVE).

The second pair of sentences is probably clearer than the first pair, because *the water* is the topic of both sentences. The passive allows the writer to keep *the water* as the topic of both sentences.

2 The passive helps the reader to focus on actions, because you can omit the agent:

Robots weld the car body together. Then the robots paint the car. Next, they clean the body.
➔ *First the car body is welded together. Then it is painted. Next it is cleaned.*

In this description of a process, the writer is interested in the actions (*welding*, *painting* and *cleaning*). The agent (*robots*) is omitted because the reader isn't interested in it (or already knows about it).

Past simple passive

The past passive uses *was/were* + past participle.

The building work	was	completed	last month.
Three skybridges	were	built	between the two towers.

The past simple passive is often used in technical writing when talking about actions or a process in the past. The reasons for using the passive are the same as for the present simple passive.

In the examples above, the agents are omitted. The writer and reader are only interested in the actions. They already know (or they aren't interested in) who did the actions.

Modal verbs v semi-modal verbs

Modal verbs. *Must* and *should* are modal verbs. They don't take *-s* in the 3rd person. They don't use *do/does* in the question or negative.

He must wear/He should wear his helmet here.
Must/Should she wear her helmet here?
He must not/should not take off his helmet here.

Semi-modal verbs. *Have to* and *need to* are semi-modal verbs. They are like modals in meaning, but have the same form as normal verbs. They take *-s* in the 3rd person. They use *do/does* in the question or negative.

He has to/needs to wear his helmet here.
Does she have to/need to wear her helmet here?
He does not have to/does not need to wear his helmet here.

The negative forms of *have to* and *need to* have a different meaning from the negatives of *must* and *should*:

Essential	Recommended	Unnecessary
You must do it. You have to do it. You need to do it.	You should do it.	You don't have to do it. You don't need to do it.
You mustn't do it.	You shouldn't do it.	

Modal verb + passive

Must, should, have to and *need to* are often followed by passive verbs in safety rules and procedures.

Your helmet	must/should		be	worn.
	has to/needs to			
Goggles	must/should/have to/need to			
	must/should	not	be	taken off.

Non-defining relative clause

In these sentences, the clauses beginning with *which* and *who* are non-defining relative clauses.

Signals are transmitted to the satellite, which then sends the signals to Earth.

John reports to Adel, who is the training manager.

The non-defining relative clause is a useful way to join two sentences together. It can be used when the word (or words) at the end of the first sentence becomes the subject of the next sentence.

Signals are transmitted to	the satellite.	then sends the signals to Earth.
	The satellite	
	the satellite, which	

| John reports to | Adel. Adel | is the training manager. |
| | Adel, who | |

Non-defining relative clauses don't provide part of a definition, or limit the meaning of the preceding word. They simply add further information. A comma is used immediately before *which/who*.

Defining relative clause

In the sentences below, the clauses beginning with *which*, *that* and *who* are defining relative clauses. They are often used in definitions. They limit the meanings of the preceding words, e.g. the thermometer in the table below isn't any kind of instrument: it's a limited type of instrument restricted to measuring temperature.

	Defining relative clause
A thermometer is an instrument	which measures temperature.
A satellite is a man-made body	that orbits the Earth.
Inventors are people	who create new devices.

Which is used with things and *who* is used with people. In defining relative clauses, *that* can replace *which* or *who*. There is no comma immediately before *which/who/that*.

Reduced relative clause

When the relative clause contains a passive, you can omit *which/that/who + is/are/was/were* without changing the meaning. The shorter relative clause is called a reduced relative clause.

| Steel is an alloy | which is | made from iron ore. |

➜ Steel is an alloy *made from iron ore.*

| LEDs are small lights | that are | found on many devices. |

➜ LEDs are small lights *found on many devices.*

| The *Titanic* was a large ship | that was | sunk by an iceberg. |

➜ The *Titanic* was a large ship *sunk by an iceberg.*

| The *Titanic* sent distress signals, | which were | picked up by the *Carpathia*. |

➜ The *Titanic* sent distress signals, *picked up by the Carpathia.*

You can reduce defining and non-defining relative clauses in this way.

Noun clause

	Noun clause	
Check Make sure/ Ensure	that	the screws are tight. your mobile is turned off.
The dial indicates The gauge tells us		the pressure has increased. the speed is too high.

Time clause

When often indicates that two actions happen in sequence, one immediately after the other:

When the spark plug ignites, the gases explode.

As often indicates that two actions happen simultaneously, both at the same time:

As the piston moves up, it compresses the fuel.

In practice, it's often difficult to decide if two actions are simultaneous or in rapid sequence. For this reason, *when* or *as* can sometimes be used with the same meaning:

When/As the brake pedal is pressed, the piston pushes the oil along the brake pipe.

Indirect *Wh-* question

Please tell me I need to know This instrument can show you The computer calculates	**Noun phrase**
	their position. your speed. the altitude of the planes.
	Indirect question
	where they are. how fast you are going. how high the planes are.

Direct questions invert the word order:
Where are they? How fast are you going?

Indirect questions don't invert the word order:
Tell me where they are. I need to know how fast you are going.

Indirect *Yes/No* question (*if/whether*)
Direct *Yes/No* questions:
Is this plastic strong? Does it break easily? Will it bend?

Indirect questions based on *Yes/No* questions:
I want to know if this plastic is strong. We want to discover whether the material breaks easily. The test will find out if the material will bend.

Noun + noun phrase
Noun + noun combinations are very common in technical English. E.g:

acceleration sensors (= sensors which measure acceleration)
vehicle crash tests (= tests which crash a vehicle to measure its safety)
a side impact crash dummy (= a dummy which measures the impact from the side in a crash)

Phrasal verbs
Phrasal verbs (e.g. *take off, pick up, take away*) are composed of two parts: verb (e.g. *take*) + adverb (e.g. *off*). They use this word order:

Imperative	Present continuous	Present perfect
Take the tyres off.	I'm taking the tyres off now.	I've taken the tyres off.
Take off the tyres.	I'm taking off the tyres now.	I've taken off the tyres.
Take them off.	I'm taking them off.	I've taken them off.
Not: ~~Take off them.~~	Not: ~~I'm taking off them.~~	Not: ~~I've taken off them.~~

Note: phrasal verbs shouldn't be confused with verbs followed by a preposition + noun/pronoun. Here are some common examples:

We climbed up the mountain. They walked through the warehouse. The car drove off the road.

In these examples, you can change the noun into a pronoun: *We climbed up it. They walked through it. The car drove off it.*

Here *up, through* and *off* are prepositions (not adverbs) and must be followed by a noun or pronoun.

Comparative adjectives
The comparative form of single-syllable adjectives ends in *-er*, e.g. *longer, wider*.
Two-syllable adjectives ending in *-y* also end in *-er*, e.g. *noisy* ➔ *noisier*.
Notice the spelling changes: *big* ➔ *bigger; wide* ➔ *wider; easy* ➔ *easier*.

When comparing two items, use *than* after the comparative adjective, e.g. *The van is higher than the car.*

There are five irregular comparatives: *better* (*good*), *worse* (*bad*), *farther/further* (*far*), *more* and *less*.

With other adjectives of more than one syllable, use *more* + adjective, e.g. *more expensive*. Use *less* with all types of adjective, e.g. *less cheap, less expensive*.

Superlative adjectives
To change the comparative into the superlative form, change *-er* to *-est, more* to *most* and *less* to *least*, e.g. *longest, widest, biggest, noisiest, most expensive, least noisy*.

The is often used in front of the superlative, e.g. *The fastest car in the world, The noisiest of the three engines.*

There are five irregular superlatives: *best, worst, farthest/furthest, most* and *least*.

Gerund: linking

You can link clauses together using verb + -ing in place of and + verb.

The heat pump extracts heat from the outside air, and transfers it into the building. ➔ *The heat pump extracts heat from the outside air, transferring it into the building.*

When a gas is compressed, it condenses, and gives out heat. ➔ *When a gas is compressed, it condenses, giving out heat.*

Past simple and past participle forms

The past participle is part of (a) the present perfect verb and (b) the passive verb. Here are some examples of verbs in this book.

Most verbs are regular. Both the past simple and the past participle end in -ed.

Be careful of the spelling changes in the words below:

Regular (ending in -ed)	
verb	past simple / past participle
activate	activated
cancel	cancelled
carry	carried
cause	caused
curve	curved
drop	dropped
fit	fitted
ignite	ignited
injure	injured
locate	located
log in	logged in
plug in	plugged in
raise	raised
receive	received
reduce	reduced
rotate	rotated
service	serviced
shape	shaped
stop	stopped
submerge	submerged
transmit	transmitted
use	used

Some verbs are irregular. The past simple and the past participle do not end in -ed.

Irregular (not ending in -ed) past simple = past participle	
verb	past simple / past participle
bend	bent
bring	brought
build	built
burn	burnt
buy	bought
cut	cut
find	found
get	got
have	had
hold	held
leave	left
let	let
lose	lost
make	made
put	put
read	read
say	said
sell	sold
send	sent
sit	sat
tell	told

Irregular (not ending in -ed) past simple ≠ past participle		
verb	past simple	past participle
become	became	become
break	broke	broken
do	did	done
drive	drove	driven
fall	fell	fallen
fly	flew	flown
go	went	gone
rise	rose	risen
run	ran	run
speak	spoke	spoken
take	took	taken
tear	tore	torn
wear	wore	worn
write	wrote	written

B Functions and notions

Method

You can talk about method (= how to do something) in these ways:

1 when the method is an action.

	Method	
The passenger activates the machine	by touching	the screen.

2 when the method is a device.

	Method	
The robot can look ahead	by using by using by means of	a camera in its head.

Questions about method: *How do you do it? How did you do it? How is it done? How was it done?*

Aim, purpose or objective

to + verb is used to talk or write about the purpose of an action.

Why do you paint the car body? To protect it from rust.
The car body is painted to protect it from rust.
The aim/purpose/objective of painting the car body is to protect it from rust.

You combine *to* with *if/whether* to state the aim or objective of a test or investigation.

Aim	*of*	Process	*is*	*to*	Verb	*if*	Phrase
The aim The purpose The objective	of	the test the investigation	is	to	find out discover	if whether	the metal bends. the plastic breaks.

Questions about aim/purpose/objective:

Why do you do it? Why did you do it? Why is this done? Why was it done? What is/was the objective/aim of doing it?

Use or function

You can talk about the use or function of a device in various ways:

Present simple

The present simple is used when you think of a machine or device itself carrying out the action, e.g. *What does the carburettor do? It mixes air and petrol.*

for + verb *-ing*

for + *-ing* are used when you think of a human agent using a tool or device, e.g. *What's this tool for? It's for hammering in nails.* This means that someone uses it to hammer in nails. *What's this (device/tool/machine) for? What do you use it for? What can you use it for? It's for producing drinking water. You use it for charging batteries. You can use it for measuring walls.*

to + verb

What's this (device) designed to do? It's designed to measure high walls. It can be used to charge batteries. You (can) use it to find lost objects.

act as + noun

You use this when the function of one object is like the function of another object, e.g. *The fan of the hovercraft acts as a propeller.*

Appearance

You can describe the shape or appearance of something in these ways:

It looks like a TV transmitter. It's shaped like a dome. It's dome-shaped. It's a dome-shaped building. It's in the shape of a dome.
It's in the shape of an L. It's L-shaped. It's an L-shaped building.
It's in the shape of a circle/triangle/square. It's circular/triangular/square in shape.

Questions about appearance: *What shape is it? What does it look like?*

Definition

When you explain the meaning of a word or technical term, you often give a definition.

Here is one very common way of forming a definition:

The thing you are defining	*be*	Type	Defining relative clause	
			pronoun	function
A thermometer	is	an instrument	which	measures temperature.
A satellite	is	a man-made body	that	orbits the Earth.
Inventors	are	people	who	create new devices.

Questions about definition: *What exactly is it? How do you define it? What's the definition of …?*

Diagnosing a problem

may, *might* and *could* are used to express a possible diagnosis.
must is used to express a certain diagnosis.
may/might/could/must + *be* are used to talk about the present.

The file	may/might/could	be	too large.	= It is possible that it is too large.
	must	be	too large.	= It is certain that it is too large.

Your firewall	may/might	be	blocking	the email	= possibility
	must	be	blocking	the email	= certainty

may/might/could/must + present perfect are used to talk about the past.

You	may/might	have	broken	it.	=	It is possible that you have broken it.
	must	have	broken	it.	=	It is certain that you have broken it.

Suggesting a solution

These are ways of suggesting a solution:
- *try* + verb + *-ing*, e.g., *Try clicking on the 'undo' button.*
- *Why don't you …?*, e.g., *Why don't you click on the 'undo' button.*
- *could*, e.g., *You could click on the 'undo' button.*

Questions asking for suggestions: *What should I do? What do you suggest I do? What do you think I should do?*

Ability

Here are some ways of expressing ability and inability when talking about properties.
- *can/cannot* + active verb: *This plastic can resist tension, but it cannot resist compression.*
- *can/cannot* + passive verb: *This steel can be stretched, but it can't be compressed.*
- suffixes *-able* and *-ible* with a passive meaning: *it's breakable = it can be broken.*

Result

These words explain the result (or effect) of something
- *As a result, Therefore* (at the beginning of a sentence)
- *and so, and therefore, and as a result* (connecting to a previous clause)

Cause

These words explain the cause of something
- *as, because, since*

You can reverse the order of the clauses, without changing the meaning:

You can touch the neutral wire without a shock, as/because/ since the system is earthed. As/Because/Since the system is earthed, you can touch the neutral wire without a shock.

Reference section

1 Abbreviations

Length

mm	millimetre(s)
cm	centimetre(s)
m	metre(s)
km	kilometre(s)

Area

mm²	square millimetre(s)
m²	square metre(s)
km²	square kilometre(s)

Volume/Capacity

mm³	cubic millimetre(s)
cm³	cubic centimetre(s)
m³	cubic metre(s)
km³	cubic kilometre(s)
ml	millilitre(s)
cl	centilitre(s)
l (or L)	litre(s)

Mass/Weight

mg	milligram(s)
g	gram(s)
kg	kilogram(s)
t	tonne(s)

Time

s	second (also **sec.**)
min	minute (also **m**, as in **rpm**)
h	hour

Electricity

A	ampere(s) or amp(s)
Ah	ampere hour(s)
W	watt(s)
kW	kilowatt(s)
kWh	kilowatt hour(s)
V	volt(s)

Temperature

°C	degree(s) Celsius
°F	degree(s) Fahrenheit

Frequency

Hz	hertz
kHz	kilohertz
MHz	megahertz
Note:	**k** (kilo = thousand) is normally lower-case
	M (mega = million) is normally upper-case
	G (giga = billion) is normally upper-case

Pressure

Pa	pascal(s)
kPa	kilopascal(s)

Force

N	newton(s)
Nm	newton metre(s) (a measurement of torque)

Sound level

dB	decibel(s)

Speed/Rate

m/s	metre(s) per second
km/s	kilometre(s) per second
km/h	kilometre(s) per hour (also) **kph**
rpm	revolution(s) per minute
bps	(heart) beats per second

Other abbreviations and units

gal	gallon(s)
pt	pint(s)
in	inch(es)
ft	foot/feet
yd	yard(s)
mi	mile(s) (also **m**)
mph	mile(s) per hour
mpg	mile(s) per gallon
gph	gallon(s) per hour
psi	pound(s) per square inch
g/km	gallon(s) per kilometre
lb	pound(s)
oz	ounce(s)
cc	cubic centimetre(s) (engine capacity)

Some other abbreviations used in this book

am	in the morning
AC	alternating current
approx.	approximately
cc	(document) copied to; cubic centimetres (engine capacity)
CCTV	closed-circuit TV
CD	compact disc
CD-ROM	compact disc, read-only-memory
CPR	cardio-pulmonary resuscitation (a procedure for someone who has stopped breathing and has no pulse)
CV	curriculum vitae, a summary of skills, qualifications and work experience
DC	direct current
DTV	digital TV
DVD	digital video disc
e.g.	for example
enc.	enclosed (or attached) document
etc.	and so on/etcetera
FAQ	frequently asked questions
Fig.	figure
FYI	for your information
GB	gigabytes
GPS	global positioning system
hp	horse power
IC	internal combustion
i.e.	that is; in other words
IP	internet protocol (as in IP address)
IT	information technology
L/kg	litres per kilogram
LNB	Low Noise Block, the feed horn on satellite dish
LPG	liquid petroleum gas
MB	megabytes
MOB	man overboard
n/a	not applicable
no.	number
pm	in the afternoon (or evening)
qty	quantity
ref.	reference/with reference to
TDC	top dead centre
USB	universal serial bus
VCR	video cassette recorder
v	versus; compared with (also **vs**)

2 Symbols

Mathematical and other symbols

+	plus; positive
−	minus; negative
x	times; multiplied by (also*)
÷	over; divided by (also/)
±	plus or minus
=	equals
≠	does not equal
>	(is) more than
<	(is) less than
≥	(is) more than or equal to
≤	(is) less than or equal to
.	point (decimal number)
n^2	n squared
n^3	n cubed
n^4	n to the power four
$\sqrt{n}$	the (square) root of n
#	hash; number
°	degree(s)

Mathematical operations

formula	description	instruction
x = n * 9/5 + 32	x equals n times 9 over 5, plus 32	to find x, multiply n by 9 over 5, and add 32
x = (n − 32)*5/9	x equals n minus 32, multiplied by 5 over 9	to find x, subtract 32 from n, and multiply by 5 over 9

Internet symbols

@	at
.com	dot com
A-B	A hyphen B (or A dash B)
A/B	A slash B (or A forward slash B)
A\B	A back slash B
A_B	A underscore B
A:B	A colon B

3 Fractions

Examples: Ten percent of the students study electronics.
Two thirds of them study electrical engineering.

$^1/_4$	(a/one) quarter	**0.25**	**25%**
$^1/_2$	(a/one) half	**0.5**	**50%**
$^3/_4$	three quarters	**0.75**	**75%**
$^1/_3$	a/one third	**0.33***	**33.3%***
$^2/_3$	two thirds	**0.67***	**66.7%***
$^1/_5$	a/one fifth	**0.2**	**20%**
$^3/_5$	three fifths	**0.6**	**60%**
$^1/_{10}$	a/one tenth	**0.1**	**10%**
$^3/_{10}$	three tenths	**0.3**	**30%**
$^1/_8$	an/one eighth	**0.125**	**12.5%**
$^7/_8$	seven eighths	**0.875**	**87.5%**
$^1/_{100}$	a/one hundredth	**0.01**	**1%**

* approximate numbers

4 British and American English

Here are some of the words used in this book, but there are many more. You can find more at the back of *Longman Technical English Level 1*. Key the words *American British English* into an internet search engine or *Wikipedia* to find more examples.

British English	**American English**
analogue	analog
block of flats	apartment building
catalogue	catalog
cross roads	intersection
crude oil	petroleum
curriculum vitae/ CV	résumé
first floor (*building*)	second floor
flat (*building*)	apartment
flyover (*roads*)	overpass
gauge	gage
gear lever (*cars*)	gear shift
ground floor (*building*)	first floor
hash mark (#)	number sign
indicators (*cars*)	turn signals, blinkers
jump leads (*cars*)	jumper cables
lift (*building*)	elevator
lorry	truck
motorway (*roads*)	freeway
petrol (*refined oil*)	gas, gasoline
roof rack (*cars*)	luggage rack
roundabout (*roads*)	traffic circle
sliproad (*roads*)	ramp
socket (*elec*)	jack, outlet
tap (*plumbing*)	faucet
traffic lights	stop lights
zed (letter Z)	zee

5 Emergency number

112 (International)

6 The Europass CV format

Key *Europass* into Google or another search engine.

7 Word parts

Note: sometimes the word parts have different meanings. Check new words in a dictionary.

Word part	Usual meaning	Example
aud-	hearing	audible
centi-	hundred	centimetre
ex-	out/out of	exhaust
frig-	cold	refrigerator
hydr-	water	hydro-electric
ign-	fire	ignition
inter-	between	internet
intra-	inside	intranet
kilo-	thousand	kilometre
-less	without	wireless
lubr-	oil	lubricate
-meter	measurement	thermometer
micro-	very small	micro-chip
mini-	small	minimum
multi-	many	multi-storey
non-	not	non-flammable
poly-	many	polytechnic
-proof	preventing	fireproof
re-	again, back	reboot
semi-	half	semicircle
sol-	sun	solar
sub-	under	submarine
super-	much greater	supertanker
tele-	distant	television
therm-	heat	thermal
trans-	across	transmit
tri-	three	tripod
ultra-	very much greater	ultra-capacitor
un-	not	uncheck
vis-	seeing	visible

Extra material

1 Action 2 Training

Task exercise 6 page 7

Find instructions for your job.

How to …
change a wheel – clean a spark plug – check the oil level

- Put the oil filler cap on.
- Clean the spark plug.
- Take out the dipstick.
- Clean the oil off the dipstick.
- Take off the spark plug cover.
- Lift up the car.
- Take out the dipstick again.
- Loosen the spark plug.
- Check the oil level.
- Lower the car.
- Loosen the wheel nuts.
- Place a jack under the car.
- Tighten the wheel nuts.
- Take off the oil filler cap.
- Put back the dipstick.
- Switch off the engine.
- Replace the spark plug in the socket.
- Add some oil (if necessary).
- Tighten the oil filler cap.
- Put the new wheel on.
- Remove the spark plug from the socket.
- Take away the jack.
- Put on the wheel nuts.
- Tighten the spark plug.
- Replace the spark plug cover.
- Take off the wheel nuts.
- Take off the old wheel.

3 Comparison 3 Equipment

Task exercise 6 page 25

Student A

You think that the Land Rover Defender is the best choice for the oil rig team. Study this information and then try to persuade your colleagues to choose this car.

Criteria	Land Rover Defender 4X4
Height	2021 mm
Passengers	9
Price	£24,700
Engine size	2.4 litre
Towing power	3500 kg
Ground clearance	215.9 mm
Max speed	132 km/h
Fuel consumption	4.7 km/L
Wheelbase	2794 mm
Tank	75 L

11 Design 2 Eco-friendly planes

Task exercise 4 page 87

Group A's design brief

You work for an international aid agency, and you specialise in appropriate technology for poor rural areas in developing countries.
Your brief is to design a simple hydro-electric power system for use in small villages. The system should be able to provide enough electricity for a group of five to eight houses using a small stream flowing down a hill of about 5 metres with a 25 degrees slope. The parts should be very inexpensive.

12 Innovation 2 Technological change

Start here exercise 3 page 92

The top 10 tools of all time, according to a survey of 3000 people:

1 knife, 2 abacus, 3 compass, 4 pencil, 5 harness, 6 scythe, 7 rifle, 8 sword, 9 glasses, 10 saw

6 Procedures 1 Safety

Task exercise 7 page 43

Student A

Work with Student B. Put all the notes together in the best order and under the correct headings. There are three procedures. Each procedure has eight steps.

- Turn off any ignition sources.
- Close all the doors behind you.
- Stay with person until emergency services arrive.
- Switch off the electricity.
- If the person is not breathing, start artificial respiration.
- Cover the person with a blanket and keep them warm.
- Leave the building by the safest route.
- Lifts must not be used.
- Evacuate the workroom and close the door behind you.
- Call Chemical Safety department.
- Call 999 to evacuate injured persons.
- Report to the assembly point.

6 Procedures 3 Directions

Speaking exercise 5 page 47

Student A

1 Student B wants to go to these places:
   - the Student Centre.
   - the Cinema.

   You are on the phone. Find out where B is now, and give directions from there. (Don't tell B that the Student Centre is point 8 on the map and that the Cinema is point 1 on the map.)

2 You want to go to these places:
   - From the North Campus entrance (E2) to the Computer Centre.
   - From the South Campus entrance (E1) to the Aeronautics Department.

   Ask Student B for directions on the phone.

Review Unit C

Exercise 10 page 51

Student A's object

Describe this object to Student B. Then check B's drawing. Does it look like your object?

8 Energy 1 Wave power

Task exercise 8 page 59

Background notes for Group 1

Read the notes about this system and prepare a presentation about it.

```
WAVE ENERGY BUOY

DEFINITION: device / wave energy → electricity
MAIN COMPONENTS: copper coil, magnetic shaft,
   fibreglass container, cable
LOCATION: copper coil in buoy floats on sea
   surface; magnetic shaft attached by cable
   to seabed
MAIN SPECIFICATIONS: buoy 4 m (H); 35 m above
   seabed; 35 m between each buoy; 1.5-3 km
   from shore; 100 kW power
OPERATION: wave oscillates → magnetic shaft
   / reciprocate (explain to listeners: this
   means 'move up and down') → shaft / move
   / through copper coil → induce / electric
   current
BENEFITS: wave energy v wind energy? more
   reliable; renewable; no fossil fuels
PROBLEM: about 500 buoys needed; could damage
   ships, fish
```

10 Forces 3 Results

Start here exercise 1 page 78

Answers:

1 unshocked, 2 shocked, 3 unshocked, 4 both shocked, 5 shocked, 6 top unshocked; bottom shocked

3 Comparison 3 Equipment

Task exercise 6 page 25

Student B

You think that the Jeep Cherokee is the best choice for the oil rig team. Study this information and then try to persuade your colleagues to choose this car.

Criteria	Jeep Cherokee 4X4
Height	1807 mm
Passengers	5
Price	£23,620
Engine size	2.8 litre
Towing power	3360 kg
Ground clearance	234 mm
Max speed	173 km/h
Fuel consumption	15.5 km/L
Wheelbase	2649 mm
Tank	77.6 L

11 Design 2 Eco-friendly planes

Task exercise 4 page 87

Group B's design brief

Driving to shops is bad for the environment and for the shopper's health. But it's difficult to do shopping on foot or cycle because of the weight and volume of shopping, and the distance from most shops. Most of the shopping trolleys for sale today are not very useful or attractive. There's a need for a 'shopping trolley' that would be strong, carry a reasonable amount of shopping and be attractive for young people to use. Design a trolley either (a) for pushing on foot or (b) for towing by bicycle.

12 Innovation 3 Vehicle safety

Task exercise 10 page 95

FACT SHEET: Rear-seat entertainment system

- allows rear-seat passengers to view DVDs
- a screen drops down from the ceiling behind the front seats
- the DVD player is mounted between the front seats
- remote controls for the DVD player, wireless headphones, and video-game controls
- system allows front-seat passengers to listen to a separate audio source while rear-seat passengers view videos

11 Design 1 Working robots

Speaking exercise 8 page 85

Student A

1 Ask Student B about their robot and make notes.

2 Read the information below and answer Student B's questions.

I'm a safety inspector for buildings, and I use the Robo Inspector for about 60% of my building inspections. It's battery-powered, weighs about 1 kg and has three wheels. It creates a strong vacuum which allows it to adhere tightly to any hard surface. It can move quickly across ceilings and climb brick walls. It carries cameras and sensors, and it looks for cracks, loose bricks and other problems. It also has a safety wire which prevents it from falling if the battery fails. Its main advantage is that it can inspect surfaces too difficult or dangerous for me to climb. The only disadvantage is that if I use two or three at the same time, they crash into each other. As a result, I suggest you should give them sensors so that they can work in teams, and track one another's position.

5 Descriptions 3 Definitions

Start here exercise 1 page 40

Answers: The four ideas were all successful in the TV show, *The Dragons' Den*.

6 Procedures 3 Directions

Speaking exercise 5 page 47

Student B

1 You want to go to these places:
   - From the North Campus entrance (E2) to the Student Centre.
   - From the South Campus entrance (E1) to the Cinema.

   Ask Student A for directions on the phone.

2 Student A wants to go to these places:
   - the Computer Centre.
   - the Aeronautics Department.

   You're on the phone. Find out where A is now, and give directions from there. (Don't tell A that the Computer Centre is point 7 on the map and that the Aeronautics Department is point 5 on the map.)

8 Energy 1 Wave power

Task exercise 8 page 59

Background notes for Group 2

Read the notes about this system and prepare a presentation about it.

```
WAVE POWER STATION

DEFINITION: device / convert energy
   from waves → electrical power
MAIN COMPONENTS: air chamber,
   turbine, generator, valves
LOCATION: fixed to the seabed;
   close to shore
MAIN SPECIFICATIONS: 35 m length x
   35 m width; 485 tonnes weight;
   made of steel; 200 m from shore
OPERATION: wave enters chamber →
   water rises and falls in chamber
   → water forces air in and out of
   hole → moving air makes turbine
   rotate → turbine turns generator
BENEFITS: free energy; no fuel
   needed; no waste produced; not
   expensive to operate
PROBLEMS: noisy; must be able to
   resist rough weather
```

11 Design 2 Eco-friendly planes

Task exercise 4 page 87

Group C's design brief

Your client has bought an old building and wants to make it into a hotel. But there is a small river along the front. The client wants you to design a small bridge to allow pedestrians to cross the river to the hotel. The river is 300 cm wide and 150 cm deep. The bridge must be able to support a maximum of five people at a time, and be wide enough for three people standing side by side. The bridge should be accessible for pushchairs and wheelchair users, so must not have steps. The surface of the bridge should be non-slip in all weather conditions. There should also be a safety device, such as a handrail, to stop people falling into the river. It should be as cheap as possible and maintenance (e.g. resurfacing or painting) should be minimal and easily completed by a non-expert.

12 Innovation 3 Vehicle safety

Speaking exercise 8 page 95

Student A

FACT SHEET: the Side Impact Protection System (SIPS)

- it cushions and protects the heads of driver and passengers in a car crash
- main parts: sensors, airbags, seat-moving mechanism
- seat-moving mechanism is located below the seats
- the airbags are located above all the side windows of the vehicle
- when sensors detect an impact, they activate the airbags
- the airbags inflate in a fraction of a second and cover the side windows
- then they deflate a few seconds later
- meanwhile, the seat is moved away from the impact danger
- sensors can detect the different sizes and weights of occupants, can detect whether seat belt is on and can detect exact location of passenger

12 Innovation 2 Technological change

Vocabulary exercise 5 page 93

Answers:

1 wheel and axle, 2 pulley and belt, 3 wedge, 4 screw, 5 lever, 6 gear, 7 rack and pinion, 8 cam and follower, 9 crank and rod, 10 ratchet and pawl

Extra material

3 Comparison
3 Equipment
Task exercise 6 page 25
Student C

You think that the Toyota Land Cruiser is the best choice for the oil rig team. Study this information and then try to persuade your colleagues to choose this car.

Criteria	Toyota Land Cruiser 4X4
Height	1830 mm
Passengers	8
Price	£28,000
Engine size	4.7 litre
Towing power	2948 kg
Ground clearance	222 mm
Max speed	174 km/h
Fuel consumption	7.2 km/L
Wheelbase	2850 mm
Tank	96.1 L

12 Innovation 3 Vehicle safety
Task exercise 10 page 95

FACT SHEET: Traction control

- prevents tyres from skidding on slippery surfaces
- sensors detect if wheels receiving power have lost traction
- sensors are mounted on drive wheels
- system automatically presses the brake many times per second to those wheels
- system also reduces engine power to wheels that are slipping

12 Innovation
1 Zero emission
Task exercise 3 page 90
Student A

Find out about hydrogen fuel cells.

FACT SHEET: the hydrogen fuel cell

- purpose of fuel cell: to generate energy from hydrogen and oxygen
- it combines hydrogen (stored in the car's fuel tank) with oxygen (from the air outside)
- it consists of two electrodes
- negative electrode (anode) is separated from the positive one (cathode) by a proton exchange membrane (PEM) made of a special polymer
- PEM lets protons pass through it, but does not let electrons through it
- a cable connects the electrodes to an external circuit
- at anode, hydrogen splits into protons and electrons
- protons go through PEM to cathode
- electrons flow round external circuit; electricity powers the car
- at cathode, hydrogen is combined with oxygen; this produces water vapour (exhaust)

Review Unit C
Exercise 10 page 51
Student B's object

Describe this object to Student A. Then check A's drawing. Does it look like your object?

5 Descriptions 2 Appearance
Start here exercise 1 page 38
Answers:

A   Plaza of the Three Powers, Brasilia, Brazil
B   Guggenheim Museum, Bilbao, Spain
C   Central Chinese Television (CCTV) Tower in Beijing, China
D   Oriental Pearl Tower, Shanghai, China
E   The Shanghai World Financial Center, Shanghai, China
F   Burj Al Arab, Dubai

11 Design 1 Working robots

Speaking exercise 8 page 85

Student B

1 Read the information below and answer Student A's questions.

2 Ask Student A about their robot and make notes.

I'm a hospital surgeon, and I use Robo Surgeon once or twice a month in my operations. I control it from a console by means of levers and a pedal in the console, which make the robot's arms and fingers move very precisely. The main strength of this robot is that it has four arms, not two, and it can operate in spaces too small for a surgeon's hands. And the robot's wrist can move through 360 degrees, which my wrist can't do. The only weakness in the design is that the camera on one arm sees only in one direction, and I have to move it around. I need to see in all directions. I would therefore suggest that the fourth arm should carry two cameras instead of one.

11 Design 2 Eco-friendly planes

Task exercise 4 page 87

Group D's design brief

Rubber car tyres are the weak link in driving safety. It's impossible to prevent punctures 100%, because any air-filled rubber container can be burst by a sharp enough object. Your brief is to design an airless tyre. It must have the same properties as a normal air-filled rubber tyre, that is, it must be flexible, deformable and elastic, it must protect the car and passengers against bumps in the road, it must have strong braking power and it must provide a smooth ride. And it has to be durable, safe and puncture-resistant.

12 Innovation 3 Vehicle safety

Task exercise 10 page 95

FACT SHEET: Night-vision assist

- allows driver to see people, animals or trees in the dark
- operates up to 350 metres ahead
- uses thermal-imaging cameras
- cameras are mounted on front of car at bottom
- camera detects object
- image is shown on display on dashboard

8 Energy 1 Wave power

Task exercise 8 page 59

Background notes for Group 3

Read the notes about this system and prepare a presentation about it.

```
WAVEROLLER

DEFINITION: device / change / wave
   energy → electricity
MAIN COMPONENTS: base plate, moving
   plate, piston pump, hydraulic pipes,
   turbine, generator
LOCATION: base plate fixed to seabed;
   hydraulic pipes on seabed; turbine and
   generator on shore
MAIN SPECIFICATIONS: moving plate
   approx. 1 m x 1 m; depth 7–15 m below
   sea surface; each plate produces 13 kW
   power
OPERATION: waves move forward and
   backward along seabed → plate
   oscillates → pistons move in
   reciprocating motion → turbine rotates
   → generator produces electricity
BENEFITS: WaveRoller invisible because
   on seabed; no noise; does not
   interfere with ships
```

Review Unit F

Exercise 9 page 99

Answers:

A This building changes shape in the wind. Each segment rotates around a central frame. The rotating segments provide a constantly changing view and also generate power.

B This is Centerfold, the world's first folding electric guitar. After you play it, you can fold it, put it in your backpack and travel easily to the next gig. You can fold it in 20 seconds.

C This boarding system for aircraft carries passengers to aeroplane doors. It allows passengers to board a plane directly from the bus, avoiding the problems of a passenger staircase, such as falls or security risks.

D This is the A-bike, invented by Sir Clive Sinclair. It is a lightweight, collapsible bike which can be folded and put into a bag. You can cycle to the station and then carry it on the train. It weighs only 5.68 kg.

3 Comparison
3 Equipment

Task exercise 6 page 25

Student D

You think that the Mitsubishi Shogun is the best choice for the oil rig team. Study this information and then try to persuade your colleagues to choose this car.

Criteria	Mitsubishi Shogun 4X4
Height	1105 mm
Passengers	5
Price	£27,300
Engine size	3.2 litre
Towing power	2800 kg
Ground clearance	225 mm
Max speed	170 km/h
Fuel consumption	12.6 km/L
Wheelbase	2545 mm
Tank	71 L

12 Innovation
3 Vehicle safety

Speaking exercise 8 page 95

Student B

FACT SHEET: the Rear Obstacle Warning System (ROWS)

- alerts driver to unseen objects behind the vehicle when reversing
- sensors and rear-view camera
- sensors in rear bumper
- camera in rear window
- sensors detect presence of nearby objects
- a tone or light signals that object is near
- tone or light changes to show distance to the object

12 Innovation 3 Vehicle safety

Speaking exercise 7 page 95

Student B

Choose one of these bio-data fact sheets, or use your own bio-data.

BIO-DATA OF MARTIN NELSON

Martin Nelson is 26, an innovation engineer at MotorSpace Company. He gained his diploma in automotive technology at Berlin Polytechnic and then a degree in automotive engineering at Poznan Technological University. He joined MotorSpace six years ago, and in that time he's designed or invented ten new products, including a new Side Impact Protection System. He's now working on a new night-vision system for cars. He plans to start his own company next year.

BIO-DATA OF DANA BRUN

Dana Brun is 27. She's a senior design engineer at Innovations Inc. After obtaining her diploma in automotive design at Lyons Technical Institute, she went on to gain her degree in systems engineering at Milan University. She's worked at Innovations for four years, during which time she's invented more than eight safety systems for cars, including a new Rear Obstacle Warning System. She's now planning to design a skid control system. She intends to stay at Innovations for at least two more years.

12 Innovation 1 Zero emission

Task exercise 3 page 90

Student B

Find out about capacitors.

Circuit A : charges the capacitor
Circuit B : discharges the capacitor and makes the flashbulb light up for a short time

FACT SHEET: the capacitor

- purpose of capacitor: to provide large amount of energy for a short time
- consists of two metal plates separated by a non-conductive material (example: plastic)
- circuit A: close switch → battery sends current to the capacitor
- capacitor holds the electrical charge, like a battery
- circuit B: close switch → capacitor sends current to flashbulb in camera
- capacitor v battery: what's the difference?
- capacitor sends its complete electric charge in a tiny fraction of a second
- battery sends its electric charge more slowly
- capacitor produces high energy, but for a short time

Speed search

Some facts about robots …

- The robots R2-D2 and C3PO are the only characters that do not change (e.g. by getting older) in all six *Star Wars* movies.
- Approximately 33% of robots in the world work on car assembly lines.
- A typical car assembly factory contains hundreds of industrial robots working on fully automated production lines, that is approximately one robot for every ten human workers.
- The Mars robots, *Spirit* and *Opportunity*, have covered over 15 km over the surface of Mars for more than three years. The designers planned them to last for only 90 days.
- More than a million industrial robots are now in use, about half of them in Japan.
- A professor of cybernetics has computer chips implanted in his left arm. He can remotely operate doors, an artificial hand, and an electronic wheelchair.

Television satellites are all in orbit about 22,200 miles (35,700 km) above the Earth and travel at approximately 7000 mph (11,000 kph). At this speed and altitude, the satellite revolves around the planet once every 24 hours, the same period of time it takes the Earth to make one full rotation. In other words, the satellite appears to be permanently at the same location. You therefore only need to direct your dish at the satellite once, and then it picks up the signal without further adjustment. Satellites transmit signals in the frequency range of 10.7–12.75 GHz (in Europe). The feed horn (or LNB, low noise block) on the satellite dish on your roof converts this high-frequency signal into a lower signal in the range of 950–2150 MHz.

WANTED

Experienced ELECTRONICS ENGINEER at Summit Elektronika

Main Duties: Responsible for a digital audio studio upgrading project. You will supervise a team of senior and junior audio technicians and maintenance staff.
Qualifications Required: a degree in electronics or audio technology
Experience Required: At least five years' experience of audio project management

Send your CV to: Summit Elektronika, PO Box 22, Berlin 10117.

A guide to job interviews Part 3: At the interview, DON'T …

- dress untidily
- be late for the interview
- be rude or impolite
- talk negatively about your previous employer
- answer only *Yes* or *No*

A guide to job interviews Part 2: At the interview, DO …

- answer every question fully
- be positive and honest about yourself
- ask questions about the job
- show your knowledge about the company
- show you are interested in the job
- talk about your ambitions

TEST RESULTS	Engine				
	A	B	C	D	E
0–40 km/h (seconds)	11.48	13.19	9.38	11.74	13.25
Top Speed (mph)	44.1	44.4	48.0	46.8	45.0
Sound Level (dB)	118	106	121	114	108
Fuel Consumption (gph)	3.6	4.1	4.5	7.5	4.0

SPECIFICATIONS	Engine				
	A	B	C	D	E
Shaft length	25 in	20 in	20 in	20 in	25 in
Engine weight	349 lb	496 lb	442 lb	370 lb	407 lb
Power	115 hp @5500 rpm				
Price	$10,000	$10,520	$9490	$8934	$9150

How it works. As a wave moves over the top of the conversion unit it depresses a disc and the force is transmitted to reciprocating pumps which deliver water to the land. The high-pressure seawater comes ashore in a narrow pipe either (1) to a turbine which produces electricity, or (2) to a reverse osmosis filter which produces fresh water.

Advantages. The first benefit is that this system uses waves and wave power, which can be found all over the world. Second, this system has a double function: it can produce electricity (via a turbine) and fresh water (using a reverse osmosis filter). Third, the energy is clean and does not use fossil fuels. Fourthly, the converter sits on the seabed, where it is invisible and safe from storms. Finally, the system does not need a large pipe system. It requires only a small diameter pipe to carry high-pressure seawater ashore.

In 1940, the Tacoma Narrows Bridge in the USA was the third longest suspension bridge in the world with the longest single span in the USA. On November 7, 1940, a strong wind blew at about 65 km per hour. The deck started moving up and down, and then from side to side. Soon the deck twisted to an angle of 45 degrees, with the result that one side of the deck was 8.5 metres higher than the other side. Next, some suspenders snapped off and a section of the bridge deck broke off from the rest of the bridge and fell into the water below. Immediately the main cable over that part of the bridge, freed of its weight, tightened like a bow string, flinging suspenders into the air like fishing lines. Then the whole of the middle section of the bridge collapsed into the water.

Afterwards, engineers tried to discover what caused the collapse. There are four main factors in bridge design: forces, materials, loads and shapes. All these factors caused the collapse of the Tacoma bridge. The wind caused a changing load on the bridge. The flat vertical face of the girder of the bridge deck created resistance to this load. This then produced a torsion (or twisting) force on the deck. The torsion was too powerful for the materials, which were not strong enough to withstand this force.

A guide to job interviews Part 1: Before the interview, DO

- find out about the company and the job
- read the job advert carefully and think how your CV matches what they want
- prepare a list of the questions you think the interviewer will ask you
- prepare a list of questions you would like to ask the interviewer

Audio script

Unit 1 Action

02

A: OK, the first thing you gotta do is bring the new wheel right up to the car. OK?

B: Yeah. I'll get it now.

A: Good. Now, the air pressure in the tyre is probably wrong, so you need to adjust it. OK? Check the pressure, then either let some air out or pump some more air in.

B: Got it. Right, I've done it.

A: Good. Now before you start lifting up the car, you must loosen the wheel nuts a bit, so get your wheel gun and loosen the nuts. … Done that?

B: Yeah, done it.

A: Right, now you're going to use the jack, so first of all put the jack under the front of the car. OK?

B: Yeah.

A: And then raise the front of the car carefully. Have you done that?

B: Yeah.

A: Right, so now take the wheel off and put it down next to you on the ground.

B: Yeah. I've done that.

A: Good. Now get the new wheel, pick it up and put it on the car. Have you done that?

B: Yes.

A: Right. Now pick up your wheel gun again and tighten up the wheel nuts. …

B: Aha. That's done.

A: Good. Now lower the car … and take the jack away.

B: Done it.

A: And of course finish off by taking the old wheel away. Just roll it away and put it over there.

B: OK.

03

1 Bring out the new tyres.
2 Lift up the front of the car.
3 Take off the two wheels.
4 Put on the new wheels.
5 Take away the old wheels.
6 Pump in the petrol.
7 Switch off all the electrical systems.
8 Turn on the emergency power source.

Unit 2 Work

04

[T = Tore; K = Ken]

T: Hi, Ken. How are things on your rig?

K: Hi, Tore. Well, we're working very hard at the moment. But I'm going on leave tomorrow.

T: That's great. Where are you going? Back home?

K: I usually go home to Nigeria. But this time I'm flying to France for a holiday.

T: Ah, fantastic. Do you work two weeks on, two weeks off?

K: No, I do three on and three off. How about you?

T: I work two two.

K: When's your next leave?

T: I'm on the helicopter right now! I'm flying to Norway!

05

1 Hi, my name's Bill, and I work in the Sub-sea crew. I'm an Assistant Sub-Sea Engineer. Basically, I repair and maintain the platform and the pipes under the sea. I report to Mike, the Sub-Sea Engineer.

2 Good morning. My name is Tore, and I'm from Norway. My job title is Assistant Crane Operator. I operate and maintain the cranes on the main deck. I report to the Crane Operator.

3 Hello, I'm Ken. I'm an Assistant Driller, and I operate the drilling equipment. I supervise the Derrick Man and the Pump Man. I report to the Driller. He's the boss.

4 Hi, my name's Adel and I'm the Chief Electrician on the rig. I maintain and repair all the electrical equipment on the rig. I supervise a team of three Electricians, and I report to the Maintenance Supervisor.

06

[T = Tore; B = Ben]

T: Hello, Deck Crew. Tore speaking.

B: Oh, hi Tore. This is Ben. How's it going?

T: Not bad. But this strong wind is a problem for the cranes. Anyway, what can I do for you?

B: I want to hold a meeting for the deck crew sometime soon.

T: OK. What's the meeting going to be about?

B: I'm going to tell them about the new safety rules for crane operators.

T: OK, that's fine. When are you having the meeting?

B: How about three o'clock next Thursday?

T: Yeah, that's great. Three o'clock next Thursday. See you then. Bye.

B: Cheers. Bye.

07

From 2003 until 2005, I worked at Comet Electronics as a technician. I left Comet in 2005 and became a full-time student at Thames Valley University in September 2005. From 2005 to 2006, I studied audio electronics at Thames Valley. In 2006, I received my Diploma in Audio Technology. Then in September 2006, I started work as an audio maintenance technician at Omega Studios.

Unit 3 Comparison

09

[S = Salesperson; C = Customer]

S: How wide is your van?

C: It's just under 1.9 metres wide.

S: OK, that's fine. The vehicle must not be wider than 2 metres.

C: Great.

S: How long is it?

C: It's exactly 7 metres long.

S: Please measure it again carefully. It must not be longer than 7 metres.

C: OK, I'll do that and get back to you.

S: How high is it?

C: It's just over 3.2 metres high, including the bicycles.

S: Mm. That's too high. The vehicle must not be higher than 2.9 metres.

C: OK, I'll take the bikes off.

10

Phone call 1

[J = Julia; MW = Mr Willard]

J: Delta Electronics. This is Customer Service, Julia speaking. How can I help you?

MW: Oh, hello. Do you sell ePhones?

J: Yes, we do. Would you like a catalogue?

MW: Yes, I would. Thanks.

J: Fine. I'll send you one right away. What's your name?

MW: Willard.

J: Sorry, could you repeat that, please?

MW: Willard.

J: How do you spell that?

MW: W-I-L-L-A-R-D.

J: And could I have your phone number, please?

MW: 0133 48655

Phone call 2

[J = Julia; MJ = Ms Jensen]

J: Delta Electronics. This is Customer Service, Julia speaking. How can I help you?

MJ: Hello. I'd like to order an ePhone, please.

J: Certainly. Which model would you like to order?

MJ: The classic one, please. The 12 GB model.

J: Fine. Could I have your name, please?

MJ: Jensen.

J: Did you say Johnson?

MJ: No, Jensen. J-E-N-S-E-N.

J: And could you give me your phone number, please?

MJ: 0288 34500

Phone call 3

[J = Julia; MW = Mr Walters]

J: Delta Electronics. This is Customer Service, Julia speaking. How can I help you?

MW: Hello. I'd like to cancel an order, please.

J: I see. Do you think you could tell me the model number, please?

MW: It was a classic ePhone, 12 GB. I ordered it by phone yesterday.

J: Right. So, do you want me to cancel it?

MW: Yes, please.

J: OK. And what's your name, please?

MW: It's Walters.

J: Could you repeat that, please?

MW: Walters.

J: Thank you. And would you mind giving me your phone number, please?

MW: It's 0987 38206.

Phone call 4

[J = Julia; MM = Ms Martinez]

J: Delta Electronics. This is Customer Service, Julia speaking. How can I help you?

MM: Er, hello. I'd like some information about the ePhone, please.

J: Certainly. What would you like to know?

MM: Well, first of all, what's the screen size?

J: Let's see. Yes, it's 88.9 millimetres.

MM: Oh, right. It's quite large.

J: Yes. Would you like me to send you a specification table?

MM: Yes, I would. Thanks.

J: Could I have your name, please?

MM: Yes, my name is Martinez.

J: Sorry, did you say Martins?

MM: No, Martinez.

J: And could I have your phone number, please?

MM: Yes, it's 9604 33887.

Phone call 5

[J = Julia; MB = Mr Brandt]

J: Delta Electronics. This is Customer Service, Julia speaking. How can I help you?

MB: Oh, hello. Yes, I bought a classic ePhone last week, and it doesn't work.

J: Oh, I'm sorry to hear that. What is the problem, exactly?

MB: I can't hear any sound.

J: Right. Shall I put you through to the service department?

MB: Yes, please.

J: OK, hold on. Could you give me your name, please?

MB: It's Brandt.

J: Could you say that again, please?

MB: Brandt.

J: Thanks. And would you mind giving me your phone number, please?

MB: Sure. It's 9977 00885.

Phone call 6

[J = Julia; MG = Ms Gray]

J: Delta Electronics. This is Customer Service, Julia speaking. How can I help you?

MG: Good morning. I wish to complain about a phone I bought from you.

J: Certainly. Would you mind telling me what the problem is?

MG: The phone doesn't work. I can't make any phone calls.

J: I'm sorry to hear that. Could you give me your name, please?

MG: Yes, my name is Gray.

J: Is that AY or EY?

MG: It's GRAY.

J: And could you tell me your phone number, please?
B: Yes, it's 3022 11816.

▶ 💿 11

A: Hello, I'd like to buy a portable radio, please.
B: Certainly. We have two colours, red or black. And there are two models. There's one with rechargeable batteries, and there's one with normal batteries. Which one would you like?
A: I'd like the red one with the rechargeable batteries, please.

Unit 4 Processes

▶ 💿 12

This monster is one of the biggest tunnel drills in the world. It's the MB471/316 Tunnel Drill, and it costs more than thirty-one million dollars. It's twenty-four point four metres long and measures about fourteen point three metres in diameter across the cutter face. It weighs two thousand tons and moves at a massive speed of three metres per hour. It needs at least two hundred and thirty workers to operate and maintain it.

Unit 5 Descriptions

▶ 💿 13

a) A: So, tell me about your invention. What's it for?
   B: It's for finding lost items.
b) A: OK. And what about this device. What's it used for?
   B: It's used for charging a flat battery from inside the car.
c) A: Tell me about this invention. What can it be used for?
   B: You can use it to move quickly over and under water.

▶ 💿 15

1 A: So, tell me all about your invention. What does it do?
   B: My invention is an electronic device which can boil eggs without using water.

2 A: So, tell me about your invention. What is it? What's it for?
   B: LifeGuard is an alarm system that can find someone who has fallen off a boat.

3 A: So, let's hear about your invention. What is it and what's its purpose?
   B: This is a music website which allows you to download and mix dance music.

4 A: So, why don't you tell me about your invention. What exactly is it for?
   B: It's a seat belt adjuster that protects children in car booster seats.

Unit 6 Procedures

▶ 💿 16

A: Right, let's brainstorm for a moment. Your diving partner is trapped under water. What do you need to do? Just come up with ideas, quickly, in any order.
B: Get his leg free from the wreckage, or rocks, or whatever.
C: We've gotta bring him up from the bottom of the sea to the surface.
D: You gotta get him OUT of the water.
A: Mm. Right, good. Any other ideas?
B: Well, you have to find him first. You need to locate him.
D: Yeah, you find him and then you've got to mark his position. Use a buoy on the surface.
C: You should give him extra oxygen, more gas, if his own oxygen is low.
A: Good, you're doing well. What else do you need to do?
D: Give him artificial respiration, if he's not breathing.
C: When he's on the surface of the sea, you have to make him float, make him buoyant.
B: When he's on the surface, you need to tow him to safety, you know, pull him to a boat or something.
A: Yeah, this is good stuff. Anything else?
B: You may have to attract help at the surface. Shout or shine a light to other boats.
C: Take him to hospital.
D: Yeah, but give him first aid, if he needs it.
A: Great. OK, let's look at these ideas again.

▶ 💿 17

A: OK, now let's look at all the ideas in this spidergram, and put them in the best order, the best sequence of events. So, let's start at the beginning. What if we don't know exactly where the diver is? If his location underwater is unknown? What should we do first?
B: We have to locate the diver, and then mark his position with a buoy on the surface.
C: And then we can cut him free, with a knife, if he's trapped.
A: Right, and what about his oxygen supply?
D: If his breathing gas is low, we have to give him some more gas. We can use an extra oxygen tank.
B: And then we should bring him up to the surface, very carefully and not too quickly.
A: Right, good, so you're at the surface, and you're holding the diver there. What if he sinks again?
C: We need to make him float, make him buoyant at the surface. We can inflate his wet suit.
D: If he's not breathing, we may have to give him artificial respiration there on the surface.
B: And call for help, if there are any other boats around. Or send a signal for help.
A: What if there's no help available? You're on the surface, but there are no other boats around?
B: Tow him to the boat, or to the land if it's close.
C: Then remove him from the water and get him into the boat or onto land.
D: If he needs immediate treatment, give him first aid.
B: And if the injury is serious, call a helicopter to take him to hospital.
A: Good, well done.

18

1

[C1 = Caller 1; R = Receptionist]

C1: Oh, hello, erm, do you think you could tell me how to get to the Engineering Department in the university?

R: Of course. Where are you at the moment?

C1: I'm driving up the M95 motorway from the South.

R: OK. Well, you have to leave the motorway at Junction 3. You'll see the sign

C1: Right. So I leave the M95 at Junction 3.

R: Yeah. Then when you come off the slip road of the motorway, you'll come to a large roundabout.

C1: OK?

R: Take the … how many? … er, the fifth exit. Yes, the fifth exit from the roundabout. One of the exits is no entry because it's a slip road from the motorway.

C1: OK. Fifth exit.

R: Then almost immediately, you'll come to the main entrance to the South Campus.

C1: Right.

R: So then, turn left into the campus and go straight ahead.

C1: OK.

R: You'll see four buildings on your left.

C1: Four buildings on my left.

R: Yes. And the Engineering Department is the last building on your left.

C1: Great. Thanks very much.

R: You're welcome.

2

[C2 = Caller 2; R = Receptionist]

C2: Hi, yeah, er, could you please tell me how to get to the Sports Centre in the university?

R: Sure. Where are you now?

C2: I'm coming out of the entrance to the South Campus.

R: Are you driving a car?

C2: Yes, I am.

R: OK … well, erm, come out of the entrance and turn right at the T-junction.

C2: OK.

R: Soon you'll come to a large roundabout over the M95 motorway.

C2: Right …?

R: Go round the roundabout, pass the no-entry slip road, and take the second main exit. You're in Comet Way. Keep going until you come to the next roundabout.

C2: OK.

R: So, turn left at this roundabout. It's the first exit. Soon you'll come to another small roundabout. There's a hotel on your left at the roundabout.

C2: OK.

R: At this roundabout, take the second exit.

C2: OK.

R: There's another roundabout ahead of you. Go straight ahead at this roundabout, second exit. Now you're going past the main entrance of the North Campus.

C2: Yeah.

R: At the next roundabout, turn left. Follow the road around to the left. You'll see the North Campus on your left.

C2: OK.

R: Just before you come to the next crossroads, you'll see a large building on your left.

C2: OK. A large building on my left. Just before the crossroads.

R: That's right. That building is the Sports Centre.

C2: Thanks. Got it!

Unit 7 Services

19

[L = Lisa; C = Caller 1]

1

L: Technical support. Lisa here. What's up?

C1: Hi, Lisa. I can't log into the network. It says WRONG PASSWORD.

L: Right. Are you sure that you're typing the correct password.

C1: The password appears automatically.

L: Oh right. You must have checked the REMEMBER PASSWORD box.

C1: Ah, yes, I have. So what do I do?

L: Uncheck the box, OK?

C1: Yes.

L: Now try typing in the correct password.

C1: Right. Yes, I've done it. I've logged in. Thanks, Lisa.

2

[L = Lisa; C2 = Caller 2]

L: Technical support. Lisa here.

C2: Oh hi, Lisa. It's Rod.

L: You again! So what's wrong now?

C2: Hi, Lisa. Yeah, sorry, it's me. Well, this time my monitor isn't working. I can't see the whole page. I can only see part of the page.

L: Aha. And are the icons and words too big?

C2: Yep. That's right.

L: OK. Well, your computer must be using the wrong screen resolution settings.

C2: Oh, right. So what should I do?

L: You should go to *Control panel*. Click on *Display*, then *Settings*.

C2: Right, I've done that …

L: Then you should move the slider up. Increase the screen resolution.

C2: OK, done it.

3

[L = Lisa; C3 = Caller 3]

L: Technical support. Lisa here. What's the problem?

C3: Hi, Lisa. Well, I can't open any email attachments.

L: OK. How about the emails themselves? Can you open them all right?

C3: Yes, the emails are fine. But when I double-click on the attachments, nothing happens.

L: Well, your email program may be blocking the attachments.

C3: Oh, right. So, what can I do?

L: Open *Tools – Options – Security*. Try lowering your security level.

C3: OK. I'll try that. Thanks.

4

[L = Lisa; C4 = Caller 4]

L: Technical support. Lisa here. How can I help?

C4: Hi, Lisa. I'm using the Internet. When I click on a link, nothing happens.

L: OK. Is it a pop-up?

C4: I don't know. It says CLICK HERE TO SEE PHOTO. But when I click I don't see the photo.

L: It may be a pop-up. Do you have a firewall?

C4: Yes.

L: OK, your firewall might be blocking the pop-ups.

C4: Right. So, what should I do now?

L: I suggest you try unblocking the pop-ups. Open your firewall program.

C4: OK, I've done that.

L: Does it say *block pop-up adverts*?

C4: Yes.

L: Try unchecking the box. Then clear your cache, refresh your web page and try again.

C4: OK, I'll try that. Thanks, Lisa.

5

[L = Lisa; C5 = Caller 5]

L: Technical support. Lisa here. What's the problem?

C5: Hi, Lisa. Yeah. Bill here. I've set up a wireless router in the next room to my computer. But I can't get a connection between the router and the computer.

L: Aha. How far is the router from the computer?

C5: It's only about eight metres away.

L: Well, another electronic device could be interfering with the connection.

C5: Oh, right. What kind of device?

L: It could be a cordless phone, a microwave oven, anything really. Do you have a cordless phone?

C5: Yes, I do.

L: It must be that.

C5: So, what should I do?

L: Well, you could move the phone away. Or why don't you move the router around? I suggest you try moving the router to a different location. Then try the connection again.

C5: OK, I'll try moving the router. Thanks, Lisa.

6

[L = Lisa; C6 = Caller 6]

L: Technical support. Lisa here. What's up?

C6: Hi, Lisa. It's Bill again.

L: Aha, hello Bill. Is it your wireless connection?

C6: Yes. I've connected my computer to the router. Thanks.

L: Good.

C6: But I can't access the Internet.

L: Is there a message on the screen?

C6: Yes. It says LITTLE OR NO CONNECTIVITY.

L: Aha. Well, it must be an IP problem. You must have given the computer a different IP address from the router.

C6: Right. So, how can I fix that?

L: Why don't you try rebooting the router first. If that doesn't work, try rebooting the computer and then the router again.

C6: OK, I'll do that. Thanks.

▶🌐 20

1 You must have checked the REMEMBER PASSWORD box.

2 Your computer must be using the wrong screen resolution settings.

3 Your email program may be blocking the attachments.

4 Your firewall might be blocking the pop-ups.

5 Another electronic device could be interfering with the connection.

6 You must have given the computer a different IP address from the router.

▶🌐 21

1 Now try typing in the correct password.

2 Try lowering your security level.

3 Well, you could move the phone away. Or why don't you move the router around?

4 I suggest you try moving the router to a different location.

▶🌐 22

[S = Steve; C = Customer]

S: Good morning, customer service. My name is Steve. How can I help you?

C: Yes, good morning. I wish to complain about a printer I bought from you.

S: Oh, I'm sorry to hear that. What exactly is the problem?

C: The AC adapter with the printer doesn't work.

S: I see. Did it work the first time you switched it on?

C: No, it didn't.

S: Well, I do apologise for that. It must be our fault. What model of printer is it?

C: It's a 3845.

S: And could I have your name, please?

C: Yes, my name is Maria Beck.

S: … And do you have your receipt there?

C: Yes.

S: That's great. Could you read out the order number, please? It's at the top on the right.

C: Errm. Yes, order number … it's 89054.

S: Great. … Right, Ms Beck. Let me just summarise the situation. You've told me that the adapter with your 3845 printer doesn't work, and has never worked. Is that correct?

C: Correct.

S: Well, I'm pleased to tell you that we will replace your adapter and the printer. You will receive the goods by the end of the week. We have your address. We'll collect the old printer at the same time.

C: Great.

S: And I'm happy to say that we're going to give you five euros discount off your next purchase.

C: That's very reasonable. Thank you.

S: You're welcome, Ms Beck. Have a nice day.

Unit 8 Energy

▶ ⊘ 23

Good morning, everyone. Today I'm going to talk about the Wave Energy Converter.

You're probably wondering what a Wave Energy Converter is. So, let's have a simple definition to start with. Very simply, a Wave Energy Converter is a system which converts the energy from sea waves into electrical power.

Before I talk about the system itself, let me tell you where it is located, because some systems are located on the surface of the sea, and some on the sea shore. But not this system. The Wave Energy Converter is fixed to the seabed.

OK, now let's look at the main components. The Wave Energy Converter has five main components or parts. These are: a very large flexible disc, a lever, a chamber which takes in sea water, a set of pistons, many sea water pipes, and of course a turbine on the land.

The main specifications of the system are as follows. The whole system on the seabed is 4.6 metres high and 20.4 metres long; the main pipe is 125 millimetres wide; the pressure of the water in the pipes is 7000 kilopascals, or 1000 psi, that's pounds per square inch. The complete system can generate 100 kilowatts of electricity.

OK, that's enough number-crunching. Let's look at how the system works. Here's a very simple account of the operation of the system. Let's start with the sea. The sea wave oscillates. This oscillating motion pushes the disc down in a linear motion. The disc makes the lever oscillate. The oscillating lever makes the pistons move in a reciprocating motion. Then the pistons push sea water from the chamber through the pipe at high pressure. The high-pressure water then makes the turbine rotate. And of course this generates electricity.

So, that's how it works. And of course this system has great benefits. The most important benefit is that wave energy is a renewable energy resource; and of course it uses no fossil fuels.

Unit 10 Forces

▶ ⊘ 25

Good afternoon everyone, and welcome. The aim of my talk today is to discuss the problem of earthquakes, the damage they cause buildings, and some solutions to this problem.

I'd like to begin by talking about what causes earthquakes. As you know, the tectonic plates on the Earth's surface have been moving for millions of years, and they're still moving. Sometimes this movement causes the surface to break. This break or fracture in the Earth's crust is called a fault. When the rock breaks, there is a sudden release of energy. Shock waves spread out through and around the Earth in all directions, starting from the focus, or epicentre, of the earthquake. At the Earth's surface the ground vibrates as the waves pass through it. This is what we call an earthquake.

And that brings me to the problem which earthquakes cause for buildings. The problem for buildings is that, during an earthquake, the ground moves in all directions.

It moves horizontally. It moves up and down. It rotates and it twists. All these movements affect buildings. But horizontal movement is the most damaging for a building. As you can see in the photograph, if a building moves too much from side to side the structure can collapse.

So, now let's move on to talk about some solutions to this problem. There are three main solutions. The first one is strengthening buildings. We do this by adding some materials, or structure, to the building to make it stronger and help it to resist the sideways movement.

▶ ⊘ 26

So, now let's move on to talk about some solutions to this problem. There are three main solutions. The first one is strengthening buildings. We do this by adding some materials or structure to the building to make it stronger and help it to resist the sideways movement.

So, let's have a very quick look at ways to strengthen a building and help it to resist an earthquake. And there are in fact six ways of strengthening a building.

The first method is the single diagonal, or brace. You have a vertical column and a horizontal beam. Then you put a diagonal brace between them at 45 degrees. This strengthens the connection between the beam and the column, as you can see in Figure 1. …

OK? So, let's move on to the second method. This is where you use two diagonals, as shown in Figure 2. The two braces cross each other. This is a much stronger way to connect a beam and a column. …

Right. Now I'd like to move on to a third method of strengthening a building. This is called a horizontal deck. As Figure 3 shows, this is a flat, horizontal plate of rigid material, usually concrete. It strengthens the vertical columns and walls. …

Is that clear? Fine. So, that brings me to the fourth method of strengthening buildings, a horizontal truss …

Unit 11 Design

▶ ⊘ 27

1

[I = Interviewer; P1 = Participant]

I: Good morning. Welcome to the Industrial Robot Convention. I hope you're enjoying it. I'm doing a survey to find out how people use robots, and what improvements can be made. Would you mind if I ask you some questions?

P1: Sure, go ahead.

I: First of all, would you mind telling me what you do, and where you work?

P1: Yes, I'm a construction engineer, and I specialise in building work on high-rise buildings and skyscrapers.

I: And what kind of robot do you use in your work?

P1: I use the SnakeBot.

I: What do you think of it. Does it help your work?

P1: Yes, if I forget to take a tool to the top of a building, I press a joystick and the SnakeBot brings it to me.

I: So, what are the advantages of the SnakeBot?

P1: Well, its main strength is that it can twist around things like girders, pipes and scaffolding. In addition, it is strong enough to carry small loads like spanners and hammers, and bring them up to me at the top of a building.

I: Excellent. So, would you say that it has any drawbacks, or disadvantages?

P1: Yes, its main weakness is that you have to control every movement with a joystick. It's a bit time-wasting, because I can't do my building work and push the joystick at the same time.

I: So, in the future, how would you suggest that it could be improved?

P1: Well, I would suggest that you should design a voice-activated SnakeBot. Then I can shout to make it climb up to me.

2

[I = Interviewer; P2 = Participant 2]

I: Hello. Welcome to the Industrial Robot Convention. I'm doing a survey to find out how people use robots, and what improvements can be made. Would you mind if I ask you some questions?

P2: I'm a bit busy. Oh all right, go on, ask away.

I: Thanks. Well, first of all, what do you do, and where do you work?

P2: I'm an emergency response worker. I search for people, and try to rescue them from under collapsed buildings, after a major disaster, such as an earthquake or explosion.

I: And which robot do you use in your work?

P2: I use the Rescue Robot.

I: What do you think of it? Does it help your work?

P2: Yes, it helps me to locate people buried under collapsed buildings.

I: So, what would you say are its main strengths?

P2: Well, I would say it has two important advantages. First of all, it can access areas which are potentially dangerous for humans to go into. It can easily move over and under things, and it can get into spaces which are too small for me to climb into. In addition to this, its camera and microphone are more sensitive than human eyes and ears.

I: So, do you think it has any drawbacks or weaknesses?

P2: Well, one thing I've noticed is that the robots are too big and heavy to climb over very large piles of rubble.

I: So, looking into the future, how do you suggest we could modify or improve it?

P2: Well, I think you need to find a way to make smaller, lighter versions of it.

I: I see. Well thanks very much indeed for sparing me your time.

P2: Don't mention it.

▶ 🎧 28

[I = Interviewer; P1 = Participant 1]

I: So, what are the advantages of the SnakeBot?

P1: Well, its main strength is that it can twist around things like girders, pipes and scaffolding.

I: Excellent. So, would you say that it has any drawbacks, or disadvantages?

P1: Yes, its main weakness is that you have to control every movement with a joystick.

I: So, in the future, how would you suggest that it could be improved?

P1: Well, I would suggest that you should design a voice-activated SnakeBot.

▶ 🎧 29

Good morning everyone, and thanks for coming.

The aim of this short presentation is to tell you about our new traction kite for cargo ships and supertankers.

I'd like to start by asking a question. Why do we need a traction kite?

Well, as we all know, cargo ships and supertankers weigh tens of thousands of tons. And the diesel oil that drives these ships is non-renewable and very expensive. We need to use less oil. So, we need to use wind energy. We need to use sails to harness that energy.

So, what is the problem with other designs for sails? Other designs use a fixed and permanent mast and sail. But this is very expensive for the ship owners, as they need to buy a new boat, or fix a mast and sail to their boats.

And that brings me to our design brief.

Our brief was to design a traction kite which is strong enough to pull a large cargo ship through the water. It must be detachable – that means it can be removed from the ship.

Now let's move on to materials. What is the traction kite made of? And what are the properties of the materials? Well, the kite is made of a special polyester. This material is tough but flexible and lightweight. It has very high tensile strength and low friction.

Right, so now let's look at the main parts of the traction kite, and their function.

As you can see in the diagram, the kite has two very large sails. These are attached to a large oval balloon. The balloon is filled with helium. A small capsule is suspended from the balloon. This capsule contains a three-man crew and computers. There are sensors on the wings. These sensors detect air pressure and air speed, and send data to the computers. The computers control the speed and direction of the kite. The kite is connected to the client ship using a strong cable.

So, how large is this kite? And how high does it fly? Let's look at some dimensions.

Well, it's a giant kite. The wingspan is 120 metres from wing tip to wing tip. The area of the sail is 5000 square metres. And it flies about 300 metres above sea level.

All right, now let's turn to the operation of the kite. How does it work?

The kite crew steer the kite to a client ship. They drop the cable to the ship, and the ship's crew attach the cable to the ship. The kite then catches the wind, and pulls the ship along with about 6000 horsepower. When the wind direction changes, or the wind drops, the kite is untied from the ship and travels to another client ship.

And finally, I'd like to mention some of the advantages of the traction kite.

The kite uses wind power, which is a renewable source. Ships which use the traction kite can use 35% less fuel on a voyage. Carbon emissions are also reduced. And the system is less expensive for the ship owners. They don't have to buy new ships with sails. They simply pay to use the kite sail when they need it.

Unit 12 Innovation

▶ 🎧 30

[P = Presenter; M = Michela]

P: Hello and welcome to the show. This week, we're looking at new car safety systems, and in the studio we have an expert on car safety, Michela Rossi. Welcome, Michela. So, let's talk first of all about the new cruise control safety system for cars. First of all, what's the full name of the system?

M: Hello Jane, and thanks for having me on the programme. Well, it's called the Smart Adaptive Cruise Control, or SACC.

P: And what's it for? What does it do exactly?

M: Well, it's a safety system, which maintains a safe distance between your car and the vehicle in front of you.

P: Why do you think we need this new system?

M: Well, you see, the statistics show that many road accidents are caused when the vehicle in front suddenly stops.

P: So, you expect this invention will prevent some of those accidents from happening?

M: Yes, that's right.

P: And what technology or principle is this invention based on?

M: It makes use of laser technology, and the principle of radar. And of course it uses sensor technology. So, you could say it's based on three technologies: lasers, radar and sensors.

P: So, the main component is a laser sensor?

M: That's right. A laser sensor and a computer which is connected to the braking and acceleration systems.

P: Where is the sensor located?

M: The sensor's mounted on the front of the vehicle. It's built into the windscreen, at the top.

P: So, tell me about its operation. How does it work?

M: Well, first of all you key in the distance you want to maintain between your car and the vehicle in front. So, if it's raining, for instance, you can key in a shorter distance. Then the system works automatically. If your car moves too close to the one in front, the sensor activates the brakes. And if your car moves too far behind, the sensor activates the accelerator a little. But you can over-ride the system by touching the brakes or acceleration pedal yourself.

P: Let's go through that step by step. You key in a distance between you and the car in front.

M: Right.

P: Then it works automatically.

M: That's right. If your car moves too close to the one in front, the sensor activates the brakes.

P: And if your car moves too far behind, the sensor activates the accelerator.

M: That's right. But you can over-ride the system. You can press the brakes or acceleration pedal yourself.

P: Well, that sounds like a great invention. Just to sum up for us, could you tell us very briefly, what are the benefits or advantages of this new invention?

M: Well, I expect it will reduce the chances of a serious accident. It's automatic, and it thinks much faster than the driver.

P: Michela Rossi, thank you very much for talking to us.

M: You're welcome.

▶ 🎧 31

A: Good morning, and welcome to the programme. Today I'm interviewing Michela Rossi, a young engineer who works for Central Motors. We'll be talking about her, and about her career in automotive technology. Good morning, Michela. And you are very young, aren't you? How old are you, exactly?

B: Good morning, Jane. Well, since you ask, I'm 24. Is that too young to be an engineer?

A: No, no, not at all. The younger the better. And how long have you worked for Central Motors?

B: I've been here for about four years now.

A: I see. So what's your job title? Inventor?

B: No, no. I'm a design engineer. I work in a team of designers and inventors.

A: And how many things have you invented?

B: I think, with the team, I've designed or invented five, no, six new products since I joined Central Motors.

A: That's fantastic. So, what qualifications do you have?

B: I have a technician's diploma from Toulouse Technical Institute and an engineering degree from the Polytechnic University of Turin.

A: Great. So, Michela, let's talk a little about your future intentions. Are you planning to invent anything else in the near future?

B: Yes, I am. In fact I'll be working on a new type of rear camera for cars. The camera will see obstructions and will warn the driver.

A: I see. And after that. What are your long-term plans for your career?

B: Ah, who knows? I'll continue working here in Central Motors for several years, I hope. Then I may start my own design company.

A: Well Michela, it's been very interesting talking to you. And good luck with your career.

B: Thanks very much.

Pearson Education Limited

Edinburgh Gate
Harlow
Essex CM20 2JE
England

and Associated Companies throughout the world.

www.pearsonlongman.com

© Pearson Education Limited 2008

The right of David Bonamy to be identified as author of this Work has been asserted by him in accordance with the Copyright, Designs and Patents Act 1988.

First published 2008

ISBN: 978-1-4058-4554-0

Set in Adobe Type Library fonts

Printed in Spain by Graficas Estella

Acknowledgements

We would like to dedicate this book to the memory of David Riley, whose tireless professionalism contributed so much to its creation and success.

The publishers and author would like to thank the following for their invaluable feedback, comments and suggestions, all of which played an important part in the development of the course: Maria Angelica Rodríguez (Instituto Luis A Huergo, Argentina) Eleanor Kenny (College of the North Atlantic, Qatar), Julian Collinson, Daniel Zeytoun Millie and Terry Sutcliffe (all from the Higher Colleges of Technology, UAE), Dr Saleh Al-Busaidi (Sultan Qaboos University, Oman), Francis McNeice, (IFOROP, France), Michaela Müller (Germany), Małgorzata Ossowska-Neumann (Gdynia Maritime University, Poland), Gordon Kite (British Council, Italy), Wolfgang Ridder (VHS der Stadt Bielefeld, Germany), Stella Jehanno (Centre d'Etude des Langues/ Centre de Formation Supérieure d'Apprentis, Chambre de Commerce et d'Industrie de l'Indre, France) and Nick Jones (Germany).

The author would like to thank Stephen Nicholl (Publisher) for his enthusiasm and dedication to the project, and for tempering his professional rigour with understanding and humour. He would also like to thank Eddi Edwards (Design Manager), Keith Shaw (Designer), Celia Bingham (Editor), Ben Greshon (Senior Editor), Kevin Brown (Picture Researcher) and Ann Oakley. Thanks also to Ian Wood for his early advice and support, and to Bruce Neale and Kate Goldrick.

The author would also like to thank his colleagues past and present around the world, the dedicated teachers of English, communication skills, science, technology, engineering, business and technical/ vocational skills, along with managers, supervisors, technicians and support staff, too many to mention, who have contributed more than they know by generously sharing their ideas and expertise. He would also like to say a special *dhanyavad* to his family and friends for their patience and unwavering support.

Illustrated by Mark Duffin, Peter Harper and HL Studios

The publisher would like to thank the following for their kind permission to reproduce their photographs:

(Key: b-bottom; c-centre; l-left; r-right; t-top)

Aaron Gold: 37cr; Alamy Images: David J. Green - energy 70 (top centre left); Ian Dagnall 38 (2); © ilian studio 70tl; Ingram Publishing (Superstock Ltd) 35; Alex Boyce - Maremmaphotos: Alex Boyce - Maremmaphotos / photographersdirect.com 24; alveyandtowers.com: 7l; Art Directors and TRIP photo Library: 38 (6); BBC Photo Library: 40; Black and Decker: 36tl; Camera Press Ltd: Alain Denantes / Gamma 65; Claudio Bacinello / Photographic Visions: 8 (sensor); Corbis: elot Alonso / Reuters 65 (bull jump); Leonard Lenz / zefa 68t; Matthew Cavanaugh / EPA 65 (tourists); Sion Touhig 65 (clock faces); Vincent Jannink / EPA 65 (man & walrus); Courtesy of Land Rover: 111; Courtesy of Toyota (GB) Ltd: 115; Daimler Chrysler: 113; David Kimber: 8 (kick start), 117; Desiree Palmen: 65 (zebra crossing); DeVillain Guitar Company, www.devillain.com: 99tc; Eye Ubiquitous / Hutchison: 7c, 7r, 8 (phone); Finis Incorporated: 37cl; Firebox.com: 49br; Fiskars Brands, Inc. UK Ltd : 37; Gear Wrench: 36c; Getty Images: Attila Kisbendek / AFP 4; Chabruken 14, 15; Christian Hoehn 56; David Oliver 96; Ron Krisel 95; Toru Yamanka / AFP 70cr; Gill Mechanical Company: 49bl; Hannes Seeberg Industrial Designer MA, www.coroflot.com/seebergdesign: 99tr; Image Quest Marine: Carlos Villoch 48; Garcia Jaulin / V & W 11 (Bill); Mark Coulin / V & W 58; John Howard Davies Photography: 8; John MacNeill Illustration: 26; Loc8tor Ltd: 36tr; LoggerHead Tools: 37r; Mark Richards Photography: 36; Matt Hazell, First Light Solutions: 49t; Michael Jantzen www.humanshelter.org: 99tl; Murata Manfacturing Co Ltd: 9; NASA: 98; PA Photos: Photocome 65 (plane); Peugeot Motor Company PLC: 112; PunchStock: Corbis 10, 11 (Ken); Digital Vision 11 (Tore), 11 (Adel), 14, 17; Image 100 12; Image Source 18; Photodisc 46; Simple Stock Shots 70 (torch); Rex Features: 38 (3); Image Source 38 (4); ISOPRESS SENEPART 65 (upsie down car); Shout Pictures 70bl; Sinopix Photo Agency Ltd 38 (5); Richard Paul Russell Ltd, www.r-p-r.co.uk: 37c; Science Photo Library Ltd: James King-Holmes / FTSS 70bl (inset); RIA NOVOSTI 66; Sinclair Research Ltd: 99br; Soundsnaps Imagery: Soundsnaps Imagery / photographersdirect.com 70 (sensor); STILL Pictures The Whole Earth Photo Library: David J. Cross 76; Structured Solutions II : 49tr; SuperStock: 52; TopFoto: 74; Transport for London: 8 (screen); Travel Ink Photo Library: David Forman 38 (1); Turbo Charge: 49cl

All other images © Pearson Education

Cover images: Front: iStockphoto: Kristian Stensoenes

Picture Research by: Kevin Brown

Every effort has been made to trace the copyright holders and we apologise in advance for any unintentional omissions. We would be pleased to insert the appropriate acknowledgement in any subsequent edition of this publication.

Designed by Keith Shaw

Project Managed by David Riley